serie oro

ROJA (a partir de 12 años)

"*Sympathy, Madness, and Crime* is a lively and well-researched contribution to the expanding body of work on women's involvement in the nineteenth-century press. Roggenkamp's focus on how newspaperwomen deployed sympathy as a professional strategy in their coverage of crime and insanity significantly expands our sense of nineteenth-century women's writing."

—**Sari Edelstein,** author of *Between the Novel and the News: The Emergence of American Women's Writing*

"Karen Roggenkamp tells the tale of nineteenth-century newspaperwomen with wit and zeal—animating their derring-do and unveiling their strategies for feminizing newspaper work. Enjoyable to read and highly teachable, *Sympathy, Madness, and Crime* explores the stories of four women who claimed controversial roles in the public sphere by insisting that journalism was consistent with womanly sensibilities. From sentiment to sensation writing, Roggenkamp argues, newspaperwomen used the rhetoric of emotional expertise to defend their professional qualifications. With fascinating anecdotes and sharp insights, Roggenkamp brings their achievements to life."

—**Catherine Keyser,** author of *Playing Smart: New York Women Writers and Modern Magazine Culture*

"Karen Roggenkamp's *Sympathy, Madness, and Crime* is a highly engaging and enormously important contribution to the fields of periodical studies and American literature. Her comparative analysis of Margaret Fuller, Fanny Fern, Elizabeth Jordan, and Nellie Bly shows that there still remains much to say about women's unique role in nineteenth-century journalism, especially their 'power of sympathy' to influence progressive reforms and the innovative genres they helped spawn. Roggenkamp's emphasis on the role of New York in their writing is also novel and insightful."

—**Mark Noonan,** Professor of English, New York City College of Technology, and author of *Reading the* Century Illustrated Monthly Magazine: *American Literature and Culture, 1870– 1893* (The Kent State University Press, 2010)

SYMPATHY, MADNESS, AND CRIME

KAREN ROGGENKAMP

Sympathy, Madness, and Crime

How Four Nineteenth-Century

Journalists Made the Newspaper

Women's Business

The Kent State
University Press
Kent, Ohio

Chapter 6 was originally published in a different form in *American Literary Realism*, vol. 40,
no. 1 © 2007 by the Board of Trustees of the University of Illinois.

Library of Congress Catalog Card Number 2016008083
ISBN 978-1-60635-287-8
Manufactured in the United States of America

Library of Congress Cataloging-in-Publication Data
Names: Roggenkamp, Karen, 1969- author.
Title: Sympathy, madness, and crime : how four nineteenth-century journalists
made the newspaper women's business / Karen Roggenkamp.
Description: Kent, Ohio : The Kent State University Press, [2016] |
Includes bibliographical references and index.
Identifiers: LCCN 2016008083 (print) | LCCN 2016014950 (ebook) | ISBN 9781606352878
(hardcover : alk. paper) | ISBN 9781631012327 (ePub) | ISBN 9781631012334 (ePDF)
Subjects: LCSH: Women journalists--United States--History--19th century. | Women in
journalism--United States--History--19th century. | Journalism--Social aspects--United
States--History--19th century. | Newspaper publishing--United States--History--19th century.
| Press--United States--History--19th century.
Classification: LCC PN4888.W66 R64 2016 (print) | LCC PN4888.W66 (ebook) |
DDC 071/.3082--dc23
LC record available at https://lccn.loc.gov/2016008083

20 19 18 17 16   5 4 3 2 1

This one is for Mason and Trevor

Contents

Acknowledgments

This book would not have been possible without the incalculable assistance of so many people and institutions, and to them I offer my profound thanks. Susan Louise Stewart, Edward Griffin, Donald Ross, J. D. Isip, and Cynthia Patterson experienced the indignity of suffering through early drafts of this book, and their suggestions yielded significant alterations to the manuscript. Jean Lee Cole and Mark Noonan, along with the anonymous reviewers for Kent State University Press, offered untold assistance with their detailed remarks and suggestions. And Joyce Harrison, acquiring editor at Kent State University Press, stood by me even though it all took far, far longer than it should have. Rest assured: I would have had it finished sooner if it hadn't been for those four meddling kids and their dog!

I also wish to thank Jacob Pichnarcik and the Interlibrary Loan department at Texas A&M University–Commerce for their incomparable efforts in acquiring the materials I required, even when they were not easily obtained—not to mention loaning me an ancient but serviceable microfilm reader when I was unable to work on campus. A Faculty Development Leave from Texas A&M University–Commerce supported the composition of this manuscript; that uninterrupted research time provided a vital boost for the progress of this book. More generally, I am eternally grateful for where I have landed professionally, because my colleagues in the Department of Literature and Language make work a pleasure and my students provide energy and hope.

Finally, my family members, including, of course, those "four meddling kids," receive more than a lion's share of my love and gratitude. You expressed (relative) patience whenever I grew overexcited about nineteenth-century periodical culture, and that forbearance is priceless in just about any context.

Introduction

Sympathy and the American Newspaper Woman

On September 3, 1859, the front page of *Frank Leslie's Illustrated Newspaper* described a surprise attack on the female editor of a Cleveland paper called the *Spy*, complete with an engraving that vividly represented the chaos in the news office (see fig. 1).[1] The anonymous "editress" had written and printed a paper "which contained some very 'spicy' articles," one of which so offended a male reader that he visited the paper's office and commenced "smashing things inanimate." Not to be intimidated, the editress, "being a woman of spirit, declared war" and "undertook to give it him wholesale." "The fun grew fast and furious," the article wryly accounts, until the man forced the woman to the ground and "went so far as to beat her with his fists" before "throwing the type out of the window" and "retir[ing], covered with glory and ink." The editress of the paper, however, "recovered in time to issue the paper as usual." Glory and ink, indeed!

This attack exemplifies, if rather dramatically, the outright hostility women might face if they dared enter the cutthroat world of the nineteenth-century newspaper marketplace, especially when such acts appeared to violate powerful ideologies about proper gender roles. From the beginning of the American republic, newspaper publishers envisioned men as their ideal readers and directed their publications toward "only literate citizens, who were

No. 196.—Vol. VIII.]   NEW YORK, SATURDAY, SEPTEMBER 3, 1859.   PRICE 6 CENTS.

DISCOMFITURE OF AN EDITRESS.

THE Baltimore *Republican*, in a late issue, contained the account of the following little affair :

It appears that the city of Cleveland, Ohio, was blessed by the weekly production of a paper called the *Spy*, which contained some very "spicy" articles, and, being edited by a female, made it its especial vocation to pry into other people's business, and to print a column or two of "personalities" in every issue ; but as the presiding spirit was of the weaker sex, the sanctum remained uninvaded until, in an evil hour, the editress animadverted in rather strong terms upon an employé on the Cleveland and Toledo Railway.

Still having some respect for the female sex, the injured individual confined himself, on his visit to the office, to smashing things inanimate ; but the editress being a woman of spirit, declared war, and, not satisfied with the ink sprinkling he had already received, undertook to give it him wholesale. The fun grew fast and furious, and the lady was at last knocked down, and in the excitement of the moment the foe even went so far as to beat her with his fists.

The noise attracted the attention of the foreman of the compositors, who came to the lady's relief, but was attacked with a hammer and put to flight, after which the railroader celebrated his triumph by smashing the furniture and presses, and throwing the type out of the window, and then retired, covered with glory and ink.

The lady was left *hors de combat* on the field, but recovered in time to issue the paper as usual.

ZURICH.

THE town of Zurich, where the Peace Conference is to be held, or has been held by the time this is read, is the capital town of the canton of the same name, and is also situated on the lake of Zurich, so celebrated for its picturesque beauty

ATTACK UPON AN EDITRESS IN CLEVELAND, OHIO.

Figure 1. *Attack upon an Editress in Cleveland, Ohio,* dramatically portrays male prejudice against a professional newspaper woman. (*Frank Leslie's Illustrated Newspaper,* September 3, 1859; author's collection)

most likely to be white and male."[2] Women, though, certainly read newspapers throughout the eighteenth and nineteenth centuries, and, even more directly, they played active, productive roles in the industry from the colonial period forward.[3] Under British rule, local printers sometimes worked alongside their wives and daughters to ensure that the business would survive the printer's death—or, on occasion, his arrest for publishing illegal materials. As Isaiah Thomas, America's first press historian, observed, it was "quite a common thing for widows . . . to take up and carry on the husband's trade, and not uncommon for them to set up businesses of their own."[4] Although many of their names are lost to time, some female printers of note survive in historical accounts, including Elizabeth Timothy, who operated and edited the *South Carolina Gazette* for seven years after her husband died in 1738 and whose business acumen Benjamin Franklin praised; Sarah and Mary Katherine Goddard, a mother-and-daughter team that ran the *Providence Gazette and Country Journal,* which Sarah Goddard's son William owned;

Clementina Rind, editor of the *Virginia Gazette,* which published Thomas Jefferson's *A Summary of the Rights of British America;* Anna Zenger, who published the *New York Weekly Journal* while her husband, Peter, was on trial for libel in 1733; and Anne Franklin, who assumed responsibility for newspapers her husband and son left her and enjoyed a printing career for twenty-three years. Indeed, America's very first printer was the widow of Joseph Glover, who died while crossing the Atlantic Ocean in 1638 with the first press for Harvard College, leaving the business of installation and operation to his capable wife.

While these early examples show women's skills in professional printing, those women who desired what we would now characterize as *reporting* roles did not, in general, benefit as the periodical marketplace grew in the nineteenth century. The numbers of newspaper titles exploded as the century progressed, but the numbers of women involved in the profession remained miniscule until the 1880s and 1890s. Between 1810 and 1825, the number of newspapers expanded from some four hundred to eight hundred titles, making the United States "by far the greatest newspaper country in the world."[5] Statistics for 1830 through 1850 are even more impressive. By 1850, the nation boasted the world's highest newspaper circulation; New York City produced 153,000 papers each day for its half million residents.[6] The growth was staggering during the next decades, and newspaper production grew fourfold between the end of the Civil War and the end of the century.

Even so, women's professional involvement in the newspaper business diminished in the early and middle decades of the century as the industry grew increasingly mechanized and professionalized, with ever-larger urban publications. Journalism historian George Douglas notes the scarcity of female journalists in the first half of the nineteenth century, despite the increase in newspaper titles. The emergence of a mass-market, penny press in the 1830s solidified women's banishment from urban papers. By the 1830s and 1840s, newspaper reporting connoted "action and power," traits "women were not ideologically supposed to possess—or at least not to display to the public."[7] Journalism historians Maurine Beasley and Sheila Gibbons remark that nineteenth-century "urbanization brought the advent of mass-circulation daily newspapers produced in grimy, noisy, downtown offices and printing plants," places "considered off-limits for women," who were expected "to conform to the prevailing ideal of 'the lady,' a genteel creature who remained at home."[8]

A few antebellum Americans did successfully carve out spaces as professional newspaper women: Cornelia Walter took over the *Boston Transcript* for her brother between 1842 and 1847; the controversial Anne Royall published her own paper, the gossipy *Paul Pry,* for twenty-three years, beginning in 1831; Ann S. Stephens was an editorial writer for the *New York Evening Express* from 1837 through 1867; Jane Swisshelm edited the *Pittsburgh Saturday Visiter,* which she founded in 1847; Grace Greenwood reported for the *New York Times* in 1852; and Lydia Maria Child edited the *Anti-Slavery Standard* and composed a weekly letter about New York events for the *Boston Courier.* An even greater number of women served as correspondents or occasional contributors, working on space rates.[9]

By the postbellum period, women experienced slightly more success in pursuing newspaper careers, aided by increasing numbers of newspapers, which were a response to industrialization, urbanization, rising literacy, and immigration. In the 1860s and 1870s, such women as Sally Joy of the *Boston Post* (later "Penelope Penfeather" of the *Boston Herald*) and Jane Cunningham ("Jennie June" Croly) of the *New York Herald* and *New York Daily Graphic* labored to push open the doors to the newsroom for subsequent generations of women. Nevertheless, overall the newspaper profession "remained the fief of men" until the end of the century.[10]

With the advent of the highly commercialized press of the late nineteenth century, media moguls like Joseph Pulitzer and William Randolph Hearst began hiring women to write pieces that might appeal specifically to female readers. Their goal was to attract advertisers, who sought access to feminine purses. Even so, most papers continued to marginalize newspaper women and encapsulate them in such roles as society and fashion reporters, or reporters of news about domestic and children's affairs. Other editors, such as Adolph Ochs of the *New York Times,* refused to hire women at all. Despite the obstacles, the number of women in the newsroom grew in the final decades of the nineteenth century. Only 35 women self-identified as editors or reporters in 1870, a number that grew to 288 in 1880, then jumped to 888 in 1890 and 2,193 (out of 30,098 journalists) in 1900, though, as pioneering newspaper reporter Elizabeth Jordan asserted, the vast majority of those women did space-work on a casual basis.[11]

As the attack on the Cleveland editress reminds us, quite colorfully, not all men welcomed the addition of female journalists to the newsroom.

As Jordan noted in 1893, throughout the nineteenth century, would-be newspaper women had "stood at the door of the sanctums, so to speak, but their invitations to enter were not urgent. Notwithstanding many claims to the contrary," Jordan complained, women in the 1890s "occupy practically the same position to-day. They are more numerous, and they are further in; but their tenure of office is distinctly open to discussion."[12] Some men stridently opposed the very idea of female reporters on ideological grounds, arguing that women's inherently emotional and refined natures rendered them useless for the newsroom. As press historian Patricia Bradley puts it, "Women were expected to be genteel creatures, but a newsroom was not a genteel place; indeed, in the views of many working reporters, it could only operate successfully if reporters eschewed the gentility that consumed the nation."[13] Edwin Shuman, in an early handbook for the profession, illustrated this attitude when he querulously asked "why any woman who can get $800 a year for teaching should wish to take up the hard work of newspaper reporting." Added Edward Bok, "A girl cannot live in the free-and-easy atmosphere of the local room or do the work required a reporter without undergoing a decline in the innate qualities of womanliness or suffering in health."[14] Other writers in the nineteenth century were equally dire in their assessments about women's abilities to perform in the newsroom or serve as anything other than society reporters. Margaret Welch, for instance, insisted in 1894 that newspaper work led to "nervous exhaustion" and possibly even death: "Two . . . women whom I have known, bright, gracious, lovely, lie to-day in untimely graves because of their labor in newspaper offices."[15] Enter the profession at your own risk, critics warned aspiring young women.

Still, enter the profession they did, and not only at the end of the century. Laboring against opponents who would deny them access to the profession, Margaret Fuller, Fanny Fern, Elizabeth Jordan, and Nellie Bly were four of the writers who sought to turn on its head the idea that women were not emotionally, intellectually, or socially equipped for journalism. In a quest for professional authority within the male-dominated world of urban, mass-media newspapers, each transformed that supposed liability into an asset, and *Sympathy, Madness, and Crime* offers a collection of case studies in how these authors deployed a rhetoric of sympathy to excavate professional space within a masculinized landscape. This book critiques, in particular, how the newspaper women wrote about a specific set of issues—insanity and criminality—as they gained and maintained professional public voices and how, in writing about mental asylums and lunatics, prisons and criminals, they buttressed their authority through a highly gendered sympathetic language. In these women's hands, sympathy yielded a powerful public tool and reinforced their expertise in one of the most restrictive segments of the nineteenth-century print marketplace.

In deploying sympathy for their articles about asylums and prisons, Margaret Fuller, writing for the *New-York Tribune* in the 1840s, and Fanny Fern, with the *New York Ledger* and other papers from the 1850s to 1870s, amplified a "womanly" language that insisted on their credentials to enter public discussions about American institutions, and the people housed within them. Through emotionally driven writing, Fuller and Fern politicized their work and produced newspaper pieces that collided domestic and marketplace concerns, "private" and "public" domains, and "female" and "male" discourses. Even as the century progressed and as professional standards of journalism shifted, newspaper women continued to channel sympathy as a productive rhetorical tool. Nellie Bly and Elizabeth Jordan, both of whom reported for the *New York World* in the 1880s and 1890s, used the feminine quality of sympathy to reinforce, sometimes paradoxically, space for themselves within the "hard news" city room of America's largest and most influential paper. Both reporters turned the idea of sympathetic fellow feeling into a journalistic credential. Yet, Bly's manipulation of sympathy differed from Jordan's and from Fuller's and Fern's as well. Where the other newspaper women in this study directed sympathy outward, toward socially dispossessed subjects, Bly's sympathies reinforced her own celebrity within the increasingly commercialized industry for which she labored, resulting in what we might call a *marketed* sympathy, which did not always translate into obvious sympathy for the abject subjects of her articles. As such, placing these four women into conversation with one another illuminates how narrative perspectives and choices persisted over time, but it also underscores some of the professional pressures and opportunities that affected women's journalistic professionalization during the nineteenth century.

For many writers in the early nineteenth century, sympathetic discourse functioned within a culture that foregrounded the ethos of sentimentalism, which had developed from eighteenth-century philosophies about sensibility. Praising the "man of sensibility" and the value of emotional identification with other individuals, writers like David Hume in *A Treatise on Human Nature* (1755) and Adam Smith in *Theory of Moral Sentiments* (1759) argued that sympathy, the "process by which people are asked to feel both like and with another person," could bridge the moral and social gulfs that lay between individuals."[16] Simply put, sympathy was "not just the capacity for feeling" but "more specifically the capacity to feel the sentiments of someone else."[17] For Smith, sympathy meant placing oneself imaginatively into the position of another, less fortunate individual and experiencing, if only for a moment, the pain of the other—that is, "fellow feeling"—and in the minds of many Enlightenment thinkers, good citizens would bear witness to the suffering of others, respond to that suffering on an individual basis, and ultimately direct private feeling into public reform. Eighteenth-century novelists gave voice to these moral and political philosophies in a style that audiences absorbed easily. Authors inscribed a "connection between vision and emotion, spectacle and sympathy" that shaped private readers into more "public" selves.[18] Readers, by entering emotionally into such novels as William Hill Brown's *The Power of Sympathy* (1789), to name just one example, were thereby encouraged to contemplate and discuss the moral, social, and political issues in the public sphere, in theory leading to necessary reform of social institutions.

Countless emotion-laden novels and stories urged their readers to bear witness to scenes of suffering and to respond by identifying with the sufferers, who were often quite different from themselves, a different social class or race, for instance. Sentimental novel reading bridged the gap between reader and subject, self and other, and the resulting emotion could lead even to more substantive social change, provided readers were moved to direct their private experience of human affinity toward social reform in order to alleviate the real-life causes of suffering that novelists had so skillfully depicted in fiction. In literature, when fellow feeling occurs among a writer, a character, and a reader, the rhetorical and literal experiences of sympathy play central roles in the joint performance, as it were, of a written text. A novel's narrator or focalizing character observes a display of suffering which motivates her or him to alleviate the conditions that cause pain, or at the very least to modify personal attitudes after viewing the scene of suffering. In turn, the reader of the scene, guided by the mediating hand of the author, observes the character or narrator experiencing the scene of pathos—and the reader, as well, through the fictionalized encounter, changes, either through direct political activism (what Hendler calls the "politics of affect") or on a more personalized, heartfelt level. The performance of sympathy, then, is "essentially mimetic" as "protagonists—and in turn, the readers who identify with them—are repeatedly presented with displays of suffering, scenes inevitably followed by demonstrations of the power of sympathy to ease pain."[19] Private feeling and public action become, ideally, one and the same.

Enlightenment thinkers had originally envisioned sentimentality, with its affective product of sympathy, as a nation-building exercise associated with both men and women, as suggested by the "man of sensibility" label. However, the rhetoric of sympathy nevertheless grew increasingly gendered as a female quality, given that it revolved, generally speaking, around an aesthetic of emotionality—a quality tied to femininity itself in nineteenth-century cultural mores and that found expression through the pervasive influence of sentimental culture. What Mary G. De Jong typifies as a "nearly universal discourse in the nineteenth century," sentimentalism valorized "feeling right," as Harriet Beecher Stowe was to proclaim famously in *Uncle Tom's Cabin.* Put another way, sentimentalism "takes as its highest values sympathy, affection, and relation," and sympathy, or "feeling right" was, as Shirley Samuels explains, "literally at the heart of nineteenth-century American culture."[20] Nineteenth-century expressions of pity and proper displays of moral behavior were values closely linked to women's ideologically inscribed place in society. As Cathy Davidson observes, "sympathy and sentimentalism . . . were increasingly considered 'female'" in the nineteenth century, and even though sentimentalism persisted throughout the century, in "postbellum America, the literary was often defined *against* sentimentality" in an attempt to remove from the public mind literature's principal association with women's writing.[21]

The idea that sentimentality and sympathy were purely feminized constructs in the nineteenth century has come under scrutiny in recent years. Hendler, for instance, questions this premise and describes his work in *Public Sentiments* as "a corrective to the long-standing tendency in scholarship on nineteenth-century American literature and culture to associate femininity with sentimentality."[22] Alice Fahs notes that men, too, produced "emotion-laden" stories, in both newspapers and fiction.[23] Likewise, scholars have problematized the concept of strictly enforced separate spheres of influence for men and women in the decades since such scholars as Barbara Welter, Nancy Cott, Mary Ryan, and Jane Tompkins published their groundbreaking studies of the ideological constructions of nineteenth-century womanhood, sentimentalism, and public and private domains, with critics stressing that the influence of men on women and vice versa was, in fact, far more complicated than earlier studies allowed.[24] The reality of that split—the so-called separate spheres paradigm, with women in the private space of the home, accompanied by the "private space" of the novel, versus men in the marketplace, with the "public space" of the newspaper—is of course complicated, and the spheres were, in reality, perfectly separate only in ideological bounds. In actual practice, "women's allegedly 'separate sphere' was affected by what men did, and how activities defined by women in their own sphere influenced and even set constraints and limitations on what men might choose to do."[25]

Nevertheless, in a study about the deployment of sympathetic discourse in the public square of the newspaper, I find merit in thinking about the paradigm of the female-centered private sphere—associated with emotion, domesticity, and submissiveness—standing against the male-centered public sphere—associated with the worlds of policy making, economics, and politics. To be sure, "private" and "public" were always, in practice, permeable categories, yet incontrovertible evidence points to cultural pressures placed on women, in particular, to remain within a private sphere of influence. Indeed, the story of sympathy in the hands of newspaper women is, in essence, one of how these women used potentially constrictive ideologies about gender in order to dismantle those very constraints. Throughout the century, critics clearly *did* associate women with both the sentimental novel and expressions of sympathy. Women were presumed inherently emotional and thus equipped for sympathetic identification, and intellectual and practical conflict arose when women, who harnessed power as a mass reading public, lacked real political power in more public spheres of influence, including government and policy making. Despite their power in the marketplace—as consumers of literature and other commodities—women continued to find themselves disenfranchised politically and economically. Literary and cultural models placed them firmly in the home, instead, reading books within the privacy of their own parlors and thereby diverting attention from the politicized public sphere. But within the literary and periodical marketplaces, women could disrupt those boundaries quite cleverly.

In the same way that scholars must disrupt overly simplified thinking about gender and sentimentality, the premise that literary sympathy would lead readers to work toward social change is likewise fraught with presumptions about sympathizers' willingness to identify with people different from themselves and to translate feeling into action. Suzanne Keen dismantles the hope that "empathic emotion motivates altruistic action" and calls "the case for altruism stemming from novel reading inconclusive at best."[26] Emotional identification can be self-serving and self-referential, subverting any personal or social reform that could potentially result from fellow feeling. Sympathizers may gravitate toward people with whom they can easily identify; sympathy will thus "reinforc[e] homogeneity" if it "relies on likeness" and "the extent" to which others "can be shown in *relation* to the reader."[27] Expressions of sympathy, furthermore, may reinforce the sympathizer's feelings of superiority to the object of sympathy. As De Jong puts it, "sentimentality could . . . go bad" if its "universalism of human feelings blocked respectful recognition of the very real differences in experience between privileged observers and the objectives of their gaze."[28] Sympathy in this case is "vampiric, as if the person of sensibility feeds on the pain of others"—as if, that is, the supposedly sympathizing observer comes to a pitiful scene with the primary or at least secondary goal of voyeuristically reveling in the pain of others, within the context of a power differential.[29]

Nevertheless, sympathy did have the power to change conditions, even if it failed to achieve its loftiest goals of fellow feeling and social improvement. Female writers called on the "discourse of compassion" "to bring about much progressive social change." The rhetoric of sympathy, embedded within "sentimentality's alliance with domestic ideology" and ideas about "women's virtue and their capacity to feel," allowed female writers—especially journalists—to "validat[e] their participation, if only by writing, in the public sphere."[30] Scholars must continue to examine the cross-fertilizing, gendered ideologies and practices of American culture to arrive at a more accurate picture of women's place—and power—in the literary and periodical marketplaces of the nineteenth century.

Ultimately, the act of sympathetic expression was envisioned as an act of power, and the public expression of sympathy—especially in the pages of the newspaper—elided literary sentimentality, associated with the "private sphere" of the feminine novel, with action, often associated with the "public sphere" of masculine influence. Reporters took their cues from the expression of sympathy in sentimental culture, not only during the antebellum period but, less directly, during the second half of the century as well, as they depicted relationships between individuals and the wider community and established the authority of the professional newspaper woman as they articulated that exchange. Fuller, Fern, Bly, and Jordan each profited from projecting a public, feminized sympathy, and each, to varying degrees, encouraged reformation not only of public institutions like asylums and prisons but implicitly of the newspaper industry, as well. A rhetoric of sympathy, that is, allowed these newspaper women to transgress professional gender lines.

I have selected Fuller, Fern, Bly, and Jordan as the hallmark figures for my study because of how their work enacts evidence of varying profession- al and sympathetic strategies and how those strategies both overlap and diverge. Thus, I deliberately limit my analysis to four relatively well-known journalists, all of whom wrote for New York papers with large circulations. These four figures were not, certainly, the only journalists who flourished professionally, or who wrote about prisons and asylums, or who deployed sympathetic discourse. Grace Greenwood, Lydia Maria Child, and Mary Mapes Dodge are just three of the better-known women who also addressed these issues in their own journalism. Even so, I contend that Fuller, Fern, Bly, and Jordan deserve continued attention, particularly in terms of how each bridged sympathy, professional concerns, and institutional scrutiny as conspicuous public authors and how their rhetorical and professional strategies overlap and diverge in significant ways. Given her position as arguably the first "professional" woman working for a mass-market daily, Fuller stands as the landmark figure for this analysis. Fern's career offers another "first," and despite the wealth of scholarship about her work, a critical gap exists in terms of how we understand her more sentimental journalistic writings. For her part, Bly wrote what was, without question, the most famous newspaper exposé of asylum life, yet placing her work into context with those other figures offers a fresh perspective on how sympathy functioned as a component of the professional class of newspaper woman that she so ably came to represent. Finally, Jordan, the least well-known of these four women, is not only a person whose work demands more atten- tion but a journalist whose own brand of professionalism counterbalances the kind of newspaper woman Bly typified. My hope is that, in examining some of the rhetorical and professional choices of these comparatively mainstream writers within a fresh critical lens, *Sympathy, Madness, and Crime* might build a framework within which—and against which—other studies of lesser-known journalists and papers might continue.

Boston and Philadelphia gave birth to the American newspaper industry, but by the early nineteenth century, New York had emerged as the unquestioned powerhouse in periodical production. Furthermore, many of the New York papers, including the ones I feature in this study—the *Tribune*, the *Ledger*, and the *World*—enjoyed significant national reach; readers across the United States subscribed to these papers, and other periodicals regularly reprinted clippings from them.[31] My investigation, therefore, pinpoints four women who shared a set of concerns, wrote for New York papers, reached enormous readerships, and became nationally conspicuous in their professional roles. In selecting these journalists, I aim to flesh out the significance of their individual work, as well as the segment of the periodical marketplace in which they circulated. Part of my motivation lies in the conviction that while a portion of the work these women produced seems well known, by reading them within a new paradigm we may gain fresh insights into larger concerns about women's professionalism, the rhetoric of sympathy, and periodical representations of asylums and prisons, as well.

This book, then, does not set out to offer a comprehensive survey of women's involvement in newspaper journalism and sympathetic discourse; my scope and purpose are more intensively focused. Nor do I wish to imply that *Sympathy, Madness, and Crime* embodies the experiences, methods, and strategies of all newspaper women in all regions of the nation and for all types and sizes of publications—and not, certainly, for all races, ethnicities, and social classes. Indeed, no single work can. The experiences of journalists from historically marginalized positions—like Ida B. Wells-Barnett and Sui Sin Far, to cite just two examples—were, by definition, different from those of Fuller, Fern, Bly, and Jordan, as were the experiences of writers for alternative papers, other regions of the nation, and other types of periodicals. To be sure, the stories of lesser-known newspaper women demand attention and a wider body of research, and a complete story of women's place in the history of American newspaper journalism will require the continued, combined efforts of many more scholars, whose work will, together, complete a picture of how women negotiated this segment of the periodical marketplace and the public sphere. The past two decades have yielded exciting scholarship about women's work in newspaper journalism, which has thus sketched in some of the shadows of that picture; studies by Alice Fahs, Jean Marie Lutes, and Sari Edelstein offer especially rich surveys of the landscape for female periodical writers in the nineteenth century. Still, the subfield of periodical studies contains much unexplored territory. In examining intensely one of the ways women used their supposed limitations—in this case, sympathy—to help clear a path toward professional legitimation, this study maps an additional portion of that landscape.

I use the term "newspaper women" to describe Fuller, Fern, Bly, and Jordan, even though their job duties differed. Critics often consider Fuller a "literary critic" and Fern a "columnist," while Bly and Jordan receive the more straightforward label of "reporter," yet the four women fulfilled, to varying degrees, reportorial roles, and "newspaper women" points to that reporting function while acknowledging that Fuller and Fern, for instance, produced additional journalism that might appear non-reportorial (such as Fuller's book reviews and Fern's imaginative sketches). I also aim to differentiate between the work Fuller, Fern, Bly, and Jordan performed and some of the other journalistic roles women more frequently filled on newspaper staffs, such as drafting society columns and contributing occasional correspondence. As John Nerone and Kevin Barnhurst observe, American newspapers started using the term "reporter" in the antebellum period, which meant "salaried or piecework employees who turned in scavenged accounts from the police courts and other such information-producing institutions." They "covered local news, concentrating on the police courts, theaters, city hall, and other regular venues." By the late nineteenth century, "these venues would become beats," and, as my study suggests, men almost exclusively filled these occupational spaces until the very end of the century. Correspondents supplemented the work of reporters; they were generally amateur or casual workers—men and, sometimes, women "whose main livelihood came from something other than newswork" and who often "wrote long informed letters" or commentary pieces "from distant places" or upon certain editorial subjects.[32]

While my methods emerge from the study of print culture and, in particular, the intertwined histories of literature and periodicals, the story of these four newspaper women is also, finally, one about female professionalism during various periods of the century; the permeable boundaries between "private" and "public"; the strategic uses of highly gendered literary constructs of sympathy; and representations of madness, crime, and institutionalization in American culture—topics that captured the interest of countless nineteenth-century Americans. My approach recasts the idea of a textual "microhistory," as revised from historiography by June Howard: a "small-scale investigation ... that begins with the particular"—in this case, the particulars of four newspaper women and their uses of sympathy in representing asylums and prisons—"in order to enter into the interconnections of things."[33] I excavate, through close readings, a particular set of articles around a shared theme, as explored by a discrete number of newspaper women who engaged with ideas about sympathetic rhetoric, in order to cast light on broader questions about the nineteenth-century journalistic and literary marketplaces, gender and professionalization, representations of public institutions, and the narrative power of sympathy. After surveying dominant representations of asylums and prisons in the periodical press, I direct attention to how Fuller and Fern configured sympathy in their writing about those issues between the 1840s and the 1870s. I then shift to Bly and consider how, through the rise of the professional female reporter and within the context of sensation-hungry new journalism in the last two decades of the nineteenth century, she manipulated the idea of sympathetic representation inside and outside of institutional walls. Finally, the lens of *Sympathy, Madness, and Crime* closes further still, to Jordan's journalistic and literary representations of a single criminal, the accused murderer Lizzie Borden. Envisioned in terms of concentric circles, my encompassing sphere involves the question of how nineteenth-century newspaper women approached the problem of professionalization, then narrows to the narrative method of sympathetic identification, tightens further to sympathy-infused representations of madness and crime, focusing on the case studies of four well-known newspaper women, and settling at last on a single case, that of Lizzie Borden.

Sympathy, Madness, and Crime opens with the contextual backdrops against which I analyze the work of Fuller, Fern, Bly, and Jordan. Chapter 1 surveys journalistic and literary representations of madness, asylums, crime, and prisons. While some writers turned a sympathetic eye toward the lunatic and criminal classes, an examination of articles published about these topics reveals a significant degree of revulsion toward and rejection of incarcerated people, in both types of institutions. These accounts serve as the journalistic and literary backdrop against which we can project how the newspaper women who dominate my study used sympathy to craft and position their own public and professional voices.

Chapter 2 turns to the earliest of the writers, Margaret Fuller, the first female journalist to work on salary for a mass-market daily paper, Horace Greeley's *New-York Tribune*. During her employment with the *Tribune*, from 1844 to 1846, Fuller established a paradigm of sympathetic expression that resonated within a wider culture of asylum- and prison-reform initiatives and within the bounds of transcendentalist philosophy. Fuller's model of sympathy, as expressed toward the residents of asylums, prisons, and half-way houses for "fallen women" who had been released from jail, rejected the coldly voyeuristic gaze more commonly directed toward incarcerated and insane women. Fuller sought, instead, an authorial—and, she hoped, readerly—gaze that turned inward, away from the abject subjects of her articles and into an exercise in self-scrutiny. She projected private pain publicly but insisted that individual readers enter into the subject of the newspaper report and in turn make their own sympathetic responses public by supporting reform movements. In displacing the boundaries between private and public in her professional role, Fuller modeled the attitudes she expected of her readers, and thus she, as a woman writing in a masculinized mass-market medium, proclaimed the efficacy of a woman's voice on the front page of the newspaper.

The next chapter looks at Fanny Fern's columns for the *New York Ledger* and other papers, published between 1852 and 1872. Comparing her reports about prisons and asylums with similar images of institutionalization and women's oppression in her novel *Ruth Hall*, I analyze Fern's use of sympathetic observation and identification, which she often conveyed with a sarcastic edge. Similar to Fuller, she examined criminal and insane Americans, and, in the process, she encouraged readers to look first upon the spectacle of their suffering and then to turn the gaze back on itself so they might reflect on their own attitudes about—and even their own culpability in—the circumstances of less fortunate women. As such, Fern likewise emphasized her authority as a professional writer, merging the private and the public, the domestic and the marketplace, the female and the male.

Chapter 4 moves to the end of the century and the famous example of Nellie Bly, who cast sympathy through the mediating prism of celebrity journalism. Writing for Joseph Pulitzer's *New York World*, Bly gained the public's eye through her undercover reporting about the Blackwell's Island insane asylum. She posed as a mad maiden, a journalistic feat that—once she emerged to tell her story of ten days in a madhouse—brought to her great fame (and to the hospital a public relations disaster) and reprised the role of "investigator" in several other exposés for the *World*, including acting as a criminal in order to investigate prison conditions from the inside. However, Bly's writing complicates the issue of reportorial sympathy. In contrast to that of Fuller, Fern, and Jordan, Bly's writing turned the picture of suffering people into a potentially entertaining spectacle, cast members in stories that featured Bly as a melodramatic heroine, worthy of the audience's sympathy. Bly's deployment and marketing of sympathy as a tool for celebrity illuminates a pivotal moment in newspaper women's professional status at the end of the nineteenth century, when the performance of daring undercover tasks and the pursuit of sensational stories allowed them to gain a foothold in the city room. Bly's work thus highlights the pressures and possibilities people like her faced in seizing market niches and serves as a useful hallmark for understanding the increasingly dramatic journalism of the late nineteenth century—and women's role in creating it.

My final chapter offers a contrast to Bly's version of sympathy by charting how Elizabeth Jordan represented a single accused criminal, the infamous Lizzie Borden, also for Pulitzer's *New York World*. Reporter, fiction writer, and magazine editor—a well-known and influential figure in her own day—Jordan covered Borden's trial for the *World* in 1893, and her writing about the case in both the newspaper and, implicitly, her fiction addresses the individual and professional power of sympathy. Her narrative framing compeled her readers to view potential murderers without the voyeurism associated with other articles about crime. In a newspaper field that presented murder as a spectator sport, Jordan's reportage insisted on critical reconsideration of the accused woman. Paradoxically, it was the emotion—the sympathy—modeled by the professional woman that resulted in superior reporting and ensured female authority in the newsroom, a theme evident in both Jordan's journalism and her fiction. At the same time, Jordan paradoxically aligned sympathy with realism and an emerging reportorial "objectivity" in order to stake a claim for her own expertise as a female journalist as news standards began to shift.

I turn now to a survey of the shared object of sympathy for the newspaper women in my study: nineteenth-century asylums and prisons and the people who resided there. By spotlighting some of the dominant representations of these institutions, we can situate the sympathetic discourses on display in the writing of Fuller, Fern, Bly, and Jordan as they confronted the public, as professionals.

CHAPTER 1

Representing Institutions

Asylums and Prisons in American Periodicals

On March 19, 1859, *Harper's Monthly* treated readers to a lengthy article, enriched with lushly detailed illustrations, depicting a journalist's visit to the insane asylum on Blackwell's Island, an engraving of which headed the piece (see fig. 2). The author of the piece, titled "A Visit to the Lunatic Asylum on Blackwell's Island," describes the inviting public grounds of the island, as well as the wards that house only mildly ill patients. But the author thirsts for more intriguing patients to view, and so, rejecting the superintending doctor's recommendation to avoid these less savory inmates, the writer insists on a tour of the "maniac wards," which contain the most unpredictable women.[1] As the doctor unlocks the door to a room full of "furious female lunatics," however, the journalist recalls "an account of an attack made by a furious maniac" in a Massachusetts institution, and he nervously surveys the patients gathered before him. "They were not pleasant to look at," he reflects. "Some wore a sleepy aspect. Some looked venomously at us. A few resembled chimpanzees." Nervousness aside, the tour proceeds calmly—at least until the journalist speaks, for then "the sound of my voice seemed to rouse them. I heard around me a buzz of strange croaking voices." Gathering his courage, the writer turns his back to the room of animalistic maniacs and hastily pursues the doctor, who has moved into another part of the ward. Even as he departs, he seems to feel one patient's "breath on the back on my neck" and expects "every instant to feel her claws there." The journalist flees the scene, convinced that "nothing but the interposition of Providence would enable me to gain the end of the corridor without a death-grapple with some of them." The *Harper's Monthly* writer, one of many who penned stories about asylum visits during the nineteenth century, had cast himself into an almost literal lion's den of insanity and lived to share it with an audience eager to stare, with horrified interest, at the beasts caged within the walls of the madhouse.

Articles about mental asylums, like that seen in *Harper's Monthly*, were surprisingly frequent in nineteenth-century magazines and newspapers, as were similar pieces about prisons. Some took as their subject a general description of these institutions, dryly detailing factual information like location, construction, population, and methods of supervision and correction. Others offered more provoking glimpses at life within the institutions, and an intimate—often invasive—peep at the people living within. A survey of some of these journalistic asylum narratives and, more briefly, prison stories delineates how periodicals shaped readers' understanding of insanity and criminality. The articles, in turn, contextualize how the newspaper women of this study approached the same subjects in authoring and authorizing their own tales. Building on the broader scaffolding of journalism's rhetorical framing of asylums and prisons, readers can better understand how Fuller, Fern, Bly, and Jordan wrote within and, often, against other cultural representations of insanity and criminality.

Reading and Reform
of the Nineteenth-Century Asylum

Fuller, Fern, Bly, and Jordan were not the only women who used sympathy in writing about public policies and institutions. Their narrative choices were consonant with other nineteenth-century women who found public voices through reform projects. Women used sympathy as a strategic tool to engage in public debates, and they did so primarily through the point of reform. Sympathetic expression was a hallmark of reform movements, including those involving prison and asylum conditions, a narrative stance that offered women a place in political discourse throughout the century. Debra Bernardi and Jill Bergman note that "benevolent activity" (and writing about that activity) "was one of the few professions available to women,"

184   HARPER'S WEEKLY.   [MARCH 19, 1859.

A VISIT TO THE LUNATIC ASYLUM ON BLACKWELL'S ISLAND.

NOTHING could have been more lovely than the morning on which I started in company with the artist, Mr. E——, to visit the Lunatic Asylum on Blackwell's Island. The thermometer stood at about 30°; but the sun was bright and warm, the air was buoyant, and after a walk of a mile or so we felt capable of any exertion.

Five years ago I visited the institutions on Blackwell's Island, and published the account of my visit in the *Herald*. On that occasion I crossed the arm of the East River which separates Blackwell's and Manhattan islands in the "Doctor's boat." That institution has now ceased to exist—the fire last winter consumed its spirit, if not its substance—and we crossed this time in the "ferry boat," the common property o, all the benevolent and penal institutions of the island. I may observe, *en passant,* that this boat, like Dr. Ranney's, is rowed by boatmen who are compulsory inmates of the Blackwell's Institutions. The ferry-boat is manned by

VIEW OF THE LUNATIC ASYLUM ON BLACKWELL'S ISLAND.

about to expire. This precaution is the more easily understood when it is borne in mind that no-

is a large scar, apparently the result of a sabre cut, the arch over the right eye projecting an inch

have something to show for the animal power under their control.

The burning of the old Penitentiary hospital was a clear gain. It was a miserable building. It is now being replaced by a fine stone edifice, built by convicts, of stone quarried by convicts from quarries on the island. The cost will thus be moderate; and the experience of the island officials is likely to insure the construction of the new building on the soundest architectural principles. The visitor is rather astonished at first at the quiet, steady manner in which the convicts work at the quarries (poor Branch was among them for some days); he asks himself why these stout fellows, with heavy hammers and drills in their hands, don't rise in rebellion and make their escape; on inquiry, however, he learns that individuals who seem to be spectators, and lounge around within easy distances of each other, are all keepers well armed, and quite prepared, in case of insubordination, to shoot down half a dozen convicts.

Figure 2. Some periodical articles about asylums included detailed illustrations, as did this engraving of the mental asylum on Blackwell's Island. (*Harper's Weekly*, March 19, 1859; author's collection)

which, coincidentally, "grant[ed] them a voice in the public sphere"—the "domestic and moral nature" of reform work "allowed women to exercise a pronounced influence over the public sphere largely because the work was associated "with the feminized private sphere."[2] Women directed a highly gendered, emotion-driven attitude toward the subjects of their reform pieces as a tool for legitimizing their work. As I note in the introduction, the question of "separate spheres" of public and private influence for women and men is a complicated and contested issue in scholarship about nineteenth-century America. However, ideologically speaking and to varying degrees across the century, gendered assumptions tied emotional expression—including displays of sympathy—to femininity, and "the privatized realm of the home" functioned as "the site and source of feeling." As Rosemarie Garland Thomson puts it, because sympathy signals "the affective bond that enables one to share another's feelings," women's reform writing "became an arena where sympathy could be both manifested and mobilized toward achieving reform and empowering women." Women used it, that is, to force public and political change. As such, sympathy "became the sentiment that legitimated" women's "entrance into and appropriation of the public sphere."[3] From prison reform, asylum reform, temperance debates, and abolitionism in the antebellum period to suffrage, education, and immigration in the progressive era, women applied their concerns about social decline to a wide range of issues. In so doing, they deployed sympathy as a wedge to widen the scope of the masculinized "public sphere," even as they stayed within proscribed gender roles.

Because "care for the indigent and sick was traditionally considered to be women's work," female reformers seized on asylums and prisons as "domestic spaces writ large," especially since moral treatment, which I describe below, functioned within the model "of a well-regulated family," living within institutional walls.[4] In the hands of some writers, asylum rooms and prison cells became oddly domestic spaces, and advocates of reform "emphasized the domestic atmosphere of the asylum" in order to ensure and justify the authority of female voices in public affairs.[5] Reformers realized that they could intervene with the governance of public institutions in the name of womanhood since they spoke "from a position of domestic, rather than overtly political, authority."[6] Unlike the bulk of articles about asylums and, in correlation, prisons—the vast majority of which were written by men—the articles that reform-minded newspaper women penned insisted on a fundamentally "feminine" way of viewing the people within these institutions. They modeled a sympathetic gaze, in contrast to the sensationalized and often dehumanizing gaze of other articles and stories, as exemplified by the *Harper's Weekly* article that opens this chapter. In the process, they amplified their own professional voices, based, paradoxically, on gendered ideas about emotion that supposedly constrained them and undermined their ability to speak about public issues within male-dominated media.

Asylums and prisons offered almost ideal locations for women to enter public conversation, especially through journalism. I look here at asylums, in particular, to illustrate my point. The number of mental hospitals—or, as they were also called in nineteenth-century popular language, insane asylums, lunatic asylums, or madhouses—skyrocketed in the early to mid-nineteenth century. America had only 18 asylums in 1840; 121 more were built by 1880, and the number increased to 300 by the early twentieth century.[7] The "typical" American asylum saw admission rise from 31 to 182 patients annually between 1820 and 1870 alone.[8] Medical professionals and the general public debated the best methods of treatment such hospitals should offer—or if they should offer treatment at all, rather than simple "warehousing"—especially in the early decades of the century, as reform efforts, spearheaded by progressive religious groups, gained traction. Beginning in the eighteenth century, English (and, later, American) Quakers, especially, championed "moral treatment" in both madhouses and prisons, calling "first and foremost to appeal to and sustain the patient's essential humanity."[9]

In the early nineteenth century, moral treatment was a preferred method at the Blackwell's Island asylum, which opened in 1839 as New York's premier mental hospital. As Samantha Boardman and George Makari explain, the asylum "was designed to be a state-of-the-art institution" that emphasized the human, rather than bestial, qualities of the mad; the need for a semblance of normalcy, such as the omission of prisonlike bars on windows, regular clothing, and what we would now recognize as occupational therapy; and the categorization and separation of patients based on type of illness. Dr. John McDonald, one of the hospital's designers, differentiated between "the noisy, destructive, and violent," "the idiots," "the convalescents," and "those in the first stages of convalescence and such incurables [who] are harmless and not possessed of bad habits."[10] An 1866 visitor to Blackwell's Island described this philosophy of care in action: "The main treatment on which reliance is placed for cure consists in sedatives and tonics, the freedom from active excitements, and the establishment of correct habits. As happiness or unhappiness in all depends upon mental training, so whatever tends to establish an evenness of temper aids not only in preventing insanity, but in actually restoring the diseased mind to its normal condition."[11]

However, public faith in asylum reform and moral treatment diminished as the century wore on and doctors failed to cure a growing population of asylum patients—and, not coincidentally, as the cost of housing patients likewise grew. David Rothman describes a "decline from rehabilitation to custodianship"—paralleled in philosophies about the treatment of criminals, as well.[12] Although the phrase "insane asylum" provoked negative reactions across the century, depictions grew even more pejorative in the 1880s and 1890s.[13]

As illustrated by print culture, Americans had always taken interest—for better or for worse—in public institutions. Articles about Blackwell's Island, the Tombs, Bellevue Hospital, New York police courts, and other asylums and correctional facilities abound in both popular and reform-oriented newspapers and magazines of the nineteenth century. Additionally, scores of fictional works depict madness and crime, often exploring fears about being wrongfully confined in asylums and prisons, a source of real horror for readers, judging by the popularity of this theme. Opinions among the general public, however, were not always in keeping with those of reform-minded individuals. Even during the period of moral treatment and positive reform movements early in the century, American readers consumed a steady diet of periodical stories that equated mental illness with violence, alongside stories about women who went insane when forsaken by lovers. Even a few of the countless, sensationalistic headlines—"An Insane Convict's Bloody Work," "Maniac Runs Amuck," "A Maniac's Deeds of Blood," "Strangled by a Maniac"—suggest the spectacular nature of such articles.[14] All too frequently, mad and bad characters served as little more than sources of superficial entertainment, opportunities to gawk at unfortunate people. Indeed, Reiss characterizes nineteenth-century psychiatry as "something of a spectator sport," and madhouses, as well as prisons, became "prominent tourist attractions ... [v]isited by those who merely wanted to gawk at the poor, the insane, and the criminal."[15] Although the idea of "asylum tourism" began much earlier in Europe—most famously with citizens paying to tour London's notorious Bethlem Hospital (Bedlam)—some American institutions, as well, found easy sources of income in the practice. Beginning with the first asylum in colonial America, visitors could "come and gape at patients as if they were animals in a zoo," though some superintendents charged entrance fees in an attempt "to discourage such visits."[16] Bloomingdale Asylum superintendent Pliny Earle, for one, spoke out against the demeaning practice: "Why should [people] visit asylums for the insane, with no higher purpose than to be amused at the freaks of an idiot or the ravings of a madman ... ?"[17]

Nevertheless, evidence of its public appeal appears frequently in American periodicals. W. H. Davenport refers in *Harper's New Monthly Magazine,* for instance, to the "sight-seer[s]" and "visitors" and "ordinary pleasure-seeker[s]" who travel to the island for general tours.[18] In fact, by the antebellum period, the practice of visiting prisons, asylums, and other institutions was well enough established that New York guidebooks and periodical articles provided detailed information about how the curious could secure tours.[19] Visitors might plan a delightful outing and even bring "picnic lunches to [the] verdant grounds" of places like Blackwell's Island.[20] One journalist explained, "Visitors are usually eager to know the cause of this or that case of insanity, and pleasure undoubtedly would be conferred by the gratification of their curiosity. Romance upon romance lies in the past of the unfortunate patients."[21] Day-trippers could satisfy their own imaginative impulses by inspecting a cast of colorful characters and constructing a plot for the helpless objects of the visitors' gaze. Americans took the desire to visit asylums with them when they traveled abroad, and they sent home accounts of asylums in other countries, which were then printed in newspapers. Likewise, European visitors to America toured asylums, most famously Alexis de Tocqueville, Charles Dickens, and Harriet Martineau.

Periodical pieces, both fictional and non-fictional, often follow a readily recognizable formula in describing asylum visits. The writer first departs for an excursion to the asylum with pleasurable anticipation, perhaps tinged with apprehension. A writer for *Lady's Home Magazine* describes a "merry party" that decides "one pleasant morning ... to investigate (if permitted) some of the mysteries" of the local asylum.[22] The 1859 *Harper's Weekly* article with which I open this chapter similarly captures the excitement of a madhouse excursion: "We, who crossed in the common ferry boat, were safely landed on the island; and after passing the inspection of certain lazy-looking and rude officials, who gave us greasy tickets certifying that we were authorized to visit the lunatic asylum, departed on our way rejoicing."[23] An 1876 *Scribner's Monthly* article, which details the sights visitors to New York must see, explains how to obtain these "cards of admission," the "greasy tickets" the 1859 article mentions.[24]

Upon arriving, the writer remarks on the institution and grounds, which sometimes appears as a gothic setting, but more frequently strikes the viewer with its idyllic and even beautiful features. An 1845 article provides precise travel directions to Blackwell's asylum and promises a delightful pastoral experience for sightseers: "You reach it by taking an omnibus or car to the Hurl Gate Ferry, and a pleasant row across, and a stroll of half a mile over the island brings you to the Asylum."[25] An article detailing an 1845 visit to the Bloomingdale hospital goes further: "It was one of the most delightful days of this season, that we were set down, after a pleasant ride, at the door of this Asylum. ... The grounds about the spacious buildings are delightfully shaded with venerable trees, and laid out with ... taste, and adorned with ... a profusion of flowers and fruit trees," belying the "wilderness of ruined minds" residing on the grounds.[26]

Once admitted within asylum walls, the writer depicts the building's structure and organization, types of therapy, daily routines, and entertainments and religious services. The visitor then moves through various hospital wards, beginning with the mild, if deluded patients, and lingering on eccentric or tragically melancholic characters in residence. Interactions with patients reveal how writers draw on literary caricatures and turn the residents of the hospitals into amusing, pathetic, or threatening figures. Articles in the *New York Times* "provided weekly running accounts of the asylum's most intriguing characters," some of whom eventually "achieved celebrity-like status."[27] Similarly, an 1866 article in *Harper's New Monthly Magazine* devotes several paragraphs to the author's amusing chat with "Mrs. Buchanan," the subject of several previous articles and the "female patient best known to the public." "Mrs. B.," as the journalist confides, "is often inquired after" by visitors to the asylum, presumably so they might engage in similarly entertaining conversations and chuckle at her delusions personally.[28] She is, in essence, a recurring character in a comic serial drama about the socially dispossessed. Almost invariably, journalists took note of the most memorable patients and sketched them as marginally fictionalized characters, like the "Tin Hat Man," the "Button Man," and the "Queen of England and the World" featured in one article.[29] One madwoman "seems to imagine herself a steam-boiler" and emits "a screech that would do honor to the whistle of the largest boat on the river"—a scene that is "extremely comical" to W. H. Davenport. A "spectator's mirth" in the comic lunatic "soon equal[s]" the mad mirth of the patients, writer Davenport assures readers, though, one can only imagine, for quite different reasons.[30]

However, amusement quickly turns to fear as the writer travels farther into the bowels of the asylum and wards for the "maniacs"—the more violent, unpredictable, and bestial patients. One reporter argues that "if a painter wished to depict the Witch Scene in Macbeth he would here find the finest models" of "all monstrosities," like the "very paragon of hideousness," a patient named Ann Barry, whose unfortunate appearance is depicted in one of the article's engravings, as well.[31] Other patients inspire stories about danger and close calls with wild beasts—what we might label the gothic lunatic. A *Harper's Weekly* article dramatizes the reporter's visit in alarming terms as a male inmate "advanced with cat-like strides" and in a moment reached "the bars which separated us. . . . Clutching them with his sinewy hands he glared at me like any tiger till I left the place. But for those bars I think he would have made an end of me."[32] Additional accounts describe the inmates as "savage beast[s]" with "swinish eyes."[33] The "imbecile and brutish" half-animals who look "less intelligent than the beasts of the field,"

FEMALE MANIACS.

Figure 3. Asylum-visit articles envisioned the mad in both pathetic and vaguely threatening terms. (*Harper's Weekly*, March 19, 1859; author's collection)

and one journalist lingers on "the awful spectacle of glaring eyes, gnashing teeth, hands working convulsively at the bars, and the sound of the most horrible yells and laughter from within."[34] Illustrations sometimes enhanced verbal descriptions of animalism, as evident in an 1859 article about Blackwell's Island, which groups together a collection of women who look more frightening than pathetic (see fig. 3).

While not all newspaper and magazine articles about asylum and prison visits were so voyeuristic, the majority of pieces throughout the century presented institutions as one more source of entertainment, akin to theaters and city parks.[35] The obvious object of these articles was to use asylum residents as a source of enjoyment rather than understanding. Many articles envisioned the real-life terrors and emotions within the asylum through literary frames, cultural shorthand that guided readers' reactions. An *Overland Monthly* journalist, for example, draws images from gothic literary convention, musing that "considered poetically, an insane asylum is like a ruined temple, where the moonlight plays on broken arches and crumbling walls, and goblin faces peer out at the windows, and strange creations flit in fantastic flight through gloomy recesses."[36] A similar construct begins an 1862 article in *Ballou's Dollar Monthly Magazine*: "It was a large gloomy-looking structure, built of dark-colored stone, supported by two heavy wings, and situated upon a gentle eminence just at the outer suburbs of the city."[37] Dozens of pieces characterize the insane in ways that deny patients' basic humanity. They typically view the people inside asylum walls with only detached sympathy, if any; their aim is spectacle, sensation, and drama—an experience akin to perusing a thrilling novel. In gazing at the residents of the madhouse, a visitor reader was, all too often, "manifest[ing] the power of one" individual "over another"—the gaze, that is, objectified the mental patient.[38]

One activity drew particular attention: so-called lunatic balls, immortalized in a three-quarter-page illustration in the December 2, 1865, issue of *Harper's Weekly* (see fig.4). As part of the moral treatment movement, asylum superintendents encouraged normalizing activities for patients, including dances, and numerous articles describe "the abject inhabitants of the asylum" as they "simulate[d] the carefree amusements of the sane." Such articles almost invariably underscore not the basic human similarities between the sane visitor and insane patient, but the marginalizing "eccentricity" of the mad.[39] Reporter Charles Coyle, for instance, describes the weekly "'crazy dance' . . . held in the chapel of the asylum." The dance provides a mirth-filled diversion for Coyle, who marvels at the odd "patients, dressed in such fantastic costumes as only a disordered fancy could arrange."[40] The author of the 1846 "Hours in a Mad-House"—obviously not an aficionado of dancing—draws similar enjoyment from his observation of an asylum dance. "The music was by a mad band!" he exclaims. "Think of that! . . . I will confess that I think dancing a very suitable amusement for the insane, and for them only. Let those who have no heads cultivate their heels."[41] Most descriptions of lunatic balls display similarly amused or bemused language, positioning the narrator as the lens through which readers can catch sight of a rather incongruous and slightly ludicrous event. Alice Maud Meadows, however, draws a more gothic tone in her description of a dance. She is at first moved to pity by the sight of the ball's participants, but pity shifts to horror as one of the asylum's "most notorious patients" approaches to ask for a dance:

> I positively shuddered. I saw advancing towards me a huge woman, with, it seemed to me, madness written in every line of her face; crafty, unreasoning cruelty in her large, prominent blue eyes; she was old, she was hideous. . . . I have seen many horrible sights in my life, but I never saw one half so horrible as that. [The asylum director] told me afterward . . . what her crimes had been. I remembered them horrifying the whole country with their unreasoning cruelty, making mothers afraid of letting their little children go out alone; and I shuddered to think that this fearful woman, this wholesale murderess of innocent children, might wish to dance with me![42]

Clearly, the association of mental illness with violence comes into sharp relief in this passage, allowing readers to experience the gothic thrill of vicarious danger, even at a madhouse ball.

Alongside straightforward journalistic accounts of asylum life, other periodical pieces flirted with the lines between artifice and reality through either subtly or overtly fictionalized stories about madness. "The Maniac's Confession," published in 1858, places its narrator on an asylum tour following "the woman in charge" as she "conducted us through various apartments." At last the tourists reach one patient, "a woman in the prime of life" and a "great beauty," who confesses that she killed her unfaithful husband in a fit of uncontrolled passion. The visit to the asylum becomes, in this tale, a didactic morality play that urges "parents [to] teach their children to control their passions."[43] More menacingly, "A Tale of Terror," merges early nineteenth-century interest in aeronautics and fascination with the "Gothic maniac." This piece describes an "aeronaut's" frustrated search for a companion to accompany him on an experimental balloon expedition. At the last moment, he agrees to take a "strange gentleman" who, as the aeronaut discovers once they are airborne, has escaped from a nearby asylum: "I was sitting in the frail car of a balloon, at least a mile above the earth, with a lunatic!"[44] Similarly, the sketch "A Fellow Passenger" shifts the

Figure 4. An article from the December 2, 1865, issue of *Harper's Weekly* pictured the frenetic—and, to many asylum visitors, entertaining—energy of "lunatic balls." (Author's collection)

locale to a remote inn, where the article's author must share a room with a stranger. Unsurprisingly, given the genre, the stranger threatens to kill the writer, on the mad "orders" of a lunatic brain. The writer narrowly avoids death and discovers later that the stranger had escaped from a Philadelphia insane asylum.[45] "A Madman's Story," "A Keeper's Story," "A Night with a Maniac," "An Encounter with a Madman"—newspapers and magazines brimmed with terrifying tales of monstrous, violent lunatics on the prowl for innocent victims who had, by mistake or happenstance, been locked up with maniacs.[46]

A similar set of stories drew on the conventions of American captivity narratives. These "wrongfully imprisoned" or "falsely committed" pieces built on fears that "persons of perfect sanity" were frequently and "unjustly imprisoned against their will."[47] Reiss points out that such tales, "virtually coincident with the rise of the asylum movement" in the 1830s and 1840s, recount the harrowing experiences of a "patient wrongfully deemed insane," who has escaped to expose the horrors of "the back asylum wards— . . . filthy, violent, raucous places where the mania of the patients is matched by the wanton sadism of the attendants." Such stories, sadly, had more than passing connection to actual, proven cases of wrongful confinement, such as when relatives locked members of their families within asylums for personal or financial gain. Some men and women published these pieces in order to expose genuine asylum abuses and to promote reform, including, most famously, Elizabeth Parsons Ware Packard, who charged that her husband had committed her to a madhouse to punish her for her religious views—not to mention her assertion of women's rights. Authors like Packard recognized that stories of abused and wrongfully committed wives could serve social and political ends. Reiss observes that "the entrance of the asylum into the plot line almost inevitably signaled the oppression of a strong-willed woman by a scheming husband or another male villain," and novelists like Fanny Fern, E. D. E. N. Southworth, and Charlotte Perkins Gilman "subtly reworked the old image of the entrapped woman in order to question the patriarchal institutions (marriage and psychiatry) that held her."[48] However, for every reform-driven story of false imprisonment, several others simply presented harrowing tales of captivity for sheer entertainment, finding an eager audience for their chilling narratives of maniacs and equally maniacal asylum doctors.

Small wonder that journalists drew on dramatic scenes, vivid characterization, and familiar literary tropes in constructing articles about their visits to asylums. Their writing was crafted to resonate in a literary marketplace that could offer its own rich supply of novels, stories, and memoirs about madness. Even a glance at some of the titles of novels about insanity and asylum life underscores the flavor of the fictional representation: *Maniac Beauty* (Osgood Bradbury, 1844), *The Wild Woman: Or, The Wrecked Heart* (Anonymous, 1864), *The Maniac, or, My Narrow Escape* (F. J. Stanton, 1879), *Driven to Madness, or, The Vengeance of a Jealous Woman* (Anonymous, 1894), *Case Number Ten, or, The Bradys and the Private Asylum Fraud: A Thrilling Detective Story* (Francis Worcester Doughty, 1899)—readers could find dozens of exciting novels to satisfy their tastes for weirdness and danger, though literary critics scoffed at the influx of lunatic-related fiction in the mid- to late nineteenth century.[49] Some journalists and critics denounced this plotline, characterizing it as a "morbid, false, mischievous" "sentiment that of late" that dominates "a fair share" of stories.[50] Likewise, a writer for *Littell's Living Age* called the use of insane characters the laziest sort of writing, a clichéd convention that weak authors seized on in their drive to create ever-more sensationalistic plotlines and improbable characters. "The very object of using such a machinery," complained the critic, "is to conceal the absence of art, the inability to invest human motives, and natural impulses, and acts, and incident such as we see around us with sufficient interest to enchain the reader."[51] But the stories sold, in droves; in the world of popular literature, the impulse to thrill overpowered artistic and social integrity quite handily.

THE BEASTLY CRIMINAL AND THE POOR PROSTITUTE

Reportage about criminality and prison life followed tracks generally parallel to those about insanity and asylums. As with the asylum reforms initiated in the 1840s, the prison reform movement drew journalistic attention as wardens like Eliza Farnham at New York's Sing Sing attempted "to [discourage] the use of corporal punishment" and to develop "more humane systems" for dealing with criminals.[52] Advocate journalists drew on sympathetic rhetoric to counter the overwhelmingly pejorative picture of crime that dominated periodical literature and pictured prisons and criminals, including prostitutes, as a dehumanized source of entertainment.

Like the harsh representations of insanity abundant in journalism and literature, the nineteenth-century print marketplace supplied a constant stream of novels, stories, and journalistic pieces that featured America's criminal element. Best-selling antebellum "urban gothic" or "city-mystery" novels by writers like George Lippard, Osgood Bradbury, and George Thompson ostensibly sought to expose the sinister underbelly of urban life with an eye toward reform; however, they so reveled in sensationalistic representations of crime that readers could easily indulge in the novels as a source of sordid pleasure.[53] Entering sympathetically into the life of the textual subject was neither the principal goal nor the end point of most city-mystery novels—nor of most newspaper and magazine articles about crime. Trivializing and objectifying stories about criminals flooded the literary landscape, journalistic and fictional alike. Throughout the entire century, starting with the penny press phenomenon in the 1830s and continuing through the new journalism of the 1880s and 1890s, the majority of successful mass-market newspapers lovingly detailed crimes—the bloodier the better—for the edification of drama-hungry readers. Those who yearned for even more dramatic, crime-focused reading could pick up specialty publications like the *National Police Gazette,* which featured the savory benefit of lurid illustration and "voyeuristic titillation."[54]

While most stories in these publications involved male criminals, those cases that featured bad women drew even more favor, and writers did not typically treat these alleged perpetrators with an eye toward sympathy. W. David Lewis notes that "popular attitudes toward female prisoners were . . . deeply affected by a belief that the consequences of delinquency and sin were more dreadful for the woman than for the man." The motives were purely ideological: "Man had reason; woman depended upon feeling. Man was designed by God for a bold and adventurous existence; woman was created for more quiet pursuits and domestic cares," forgiving attitudes on display in the reformist articles I describe above (and in the writings of Fuller and Fern). If a woman engaged in criminal acts, she "had gone against her very nature" and "thrown aside her natural sentiments and feelings," and "only a miracle could ever restore her to a proper course," especially if she had fallen sexually. In the face of such attitudes, as reinforced by constant articles in wildly popular urban papers, reformers "faced great difficulty in overcoming harsh public attitudes," since "many upright citizens believed" prostitutes were "outside the pale of sympathy."[55] Compassionate views seemed naïve, unrealistic—even weak and womanly.

Still, some female journalists and fiction writers published compassionate pieces about prisons and the people confined within them. As I discuss in the following chapters, one of the most consistent assertions both Fuller and Fern make in their writings about criminals, including prostitutes, is that people are driven to crime because of social forces beyond their control, especially poverty. Following this line of reasoning, when Fuller and Fern wrote about incarcerated prostitutes, in particular, they joined many other female reformist journalists in promoting a picture of "the innocent prostitute" or "the seduced prostitute."[56] In fact, sympathetic writers sometimes linked insanity to sexual exploitation. One asylum administrator noted in 1859, for instance, that "the bulk of his female patients were immigrant girls (chiefly Irish) who had been deluded, seduced, cheated, and otherwise ill-used on arrival here; and who, on realizing their miserable condition, had gone mad from the shock of the disappointment."[57] Sympathetic depictions of criminal women most frequently appeared in class-infused discussions of prostitution, which was "a subject of particular public attention" in the antebellum period and which journalists and fiction-writers sometimes linked not to female depravity but to the theory that prostitution could almost invariably "be traced back to a male seducer," resulting in what I term "the seduced prostitute." As Karen Renner notes, "in fictional depictions and nonfictional investigations alike, seduction came to be considered a typical precursory event in the life story of the prostitute, one that transformed a woman who could be seen as an active deviant into a victim."[58]

Articles about imprisoned prostitutes strove to establish this transformation by inviting readers to enter the textual scene intimately, establishing a bond of fellow feeling with incarcerated women. The author of "A Sabbath Scene on Blackwell's Island," for example, asks readers to "go in" to the penitentiary "and join in the worship" underway in the chapel.[59] As the convicted prostitutes file into the chapel, the author "giv[es] way to [her] feelings" and recognizes the women as, in effect, her mothers and sisters—women who "have a woman's heart within them." Instead of casting a judgmental eye on the convicts, the author asks how the "thousands of females, orphaned, homeless, and friendless" are to live if they choose "a slow, lingering death from absolute want" over prostitution. They may have sinned, but "have not these women, in the first instance, been sinned against? have they not been wronged?" The writer finishes the short piece with yet another attempt to place the reader into the penitentiary room and to "hear" the women as they sing their songs of mingled remorse and righteousness.[60]

Prisoner's Friend, a reformist paper, offered a comparably sympathetic construction in an 1849 article detailing the reporter's visit to The Tombs, which the author characterizes as a "grim mausoleum of Hope!" and a "foul lazar-house of polluted and festering Humanity!" In language akin to that used by the narrator of Rebecca Harding Davis's "Life in the Iron Mills," the journalist commands the reader, "Let us enter by a side door, and explore from the ground upward." The sight of female prisoners waiting to appear before the judge, "crammed into a long lampless corridor" and "[lying] huddled up in their rages against the bare stone wall, or rav[ing] in hideous fury to and fro" chills the observer. The article implies that print representations of criminals tempt the public to view the prisoners as cultural outsiders, for many are "drunken, bloated, diseased" creatures who are "cursing and blaspheming."[61] Stop, the narrator commands, and "remember that all these monstrous creatures were born with pure, womanly souls, and that the chances are nine hundred and ninety-nine in a thousand, that they are driven to their present condition by starvation and the wiles of some heartless man-villain, and that they alone are punished while the man goes free."[62]

In her own account of a visit, Lydia Maria Child echoes the accusations laid out in *Prisoner's Friend*. Within the Blackwell's Island prison, she notes in *Letters from New-York*, "more than half the inmates" are women, and "of course a large proportion of them were taken up as 'street-walkers.'"[63] In Child's eyes, however, these women are victims. The true criminals are the "men who made them such, who, perchance, caused the love of a human heart to be its ruin, and changed tenderness into sensuality and crime"—men, she charges, who may even now be "sit[ting] in council in the City Hall and pass[ing] 'regulations' to clear the streets they have filled with sin." Child also blames the risqué "flash press" for turning crime into sensational reading and, by extension, cultivating an atmosphere in which even more crime can flourish. These "polluted publications" are to blame for "circulating a paper as immoral, and perhaps more dangerous" than the common criminal, yet reporters for licentious papers are free to roam the halls of The Tombs, on the prowl for sensationalistic stories.[64] Periodicals have created a picture of depravity and degeneracy for the pleasure of debased readers; small wonder that the public would, in turn, view the people who fall into that depravity in less than sympathetic terms.

The plethora of articles, stories, sketches, and novels about insanity and crime—only a fraction of which appear here—reflect the intense and often problematic public interest in these topics. Adding their own perspectives to the subject, Fuller, Fern, Bly, and Jordan provided readers with the opportunity to adventure vicariously into intimidating and potentially dangerous spaces and to see for themselves, through the pages of mass-market periodicals, the cultural outsiders who might otherwise exist only in fanciful and distorted imagination. Examination of these articles, however, offers more than a picture of life for criminals and madmen. Their work also offers a picture of how newspaper women actively crafted their own professional space in the act of engaging with marginalized citizens.

CHAPTER 2

Scenes of Sympathy

Margaret Fuller's *New-York Tribune* Reportage

Were all this right in the private sphere, the public would soon right itself.
—Margaret Fuller, "Christmas," *New-York Tribune,* December 25, 1844

In her 1845 treatise *Woman in the Nineteenth Century,* Margaret Fuller famously proposes a "ravishing harmony of the spheres." In startling language, she rejects the overly simplistic ideological formulation of man as "head" and woman "heart," pushing instead for a democracy whose citizens might refute the notion that women, as well as men, are suited for a single sphere of influence. "Women have taken possession of so many provinces for which men had pronounced them unfit," including authorship, Fuller proclaims, and in that possession she envisions a new era in which women will speak powerfully, in public. Pointing to the example of reformers Angelina Grimké and Abby Kelley, Fuller argues that women who project their voices into public arenas "invariably subdue the prejudices of their hearers and excite an interest proportionate to the aversion with which it had been the purpose to regard them."[1] Women who use the public stage to address wide, co-gendered audiences can provoke change, both within the individual listeners and, by implication, within the broader community as well.

From 1844 to 1846, Fuller learned firsthand the benefit of claiming "provinces for which men had pronounced [her] unfit" and of establishing a bold public voice, for it was then that *New-York Tribune* editor Horace Greeley hired her, at a salary of $500 per year, as a full-time newspaper writer, literary critic, and, eventually, foreign correspondent.[2] By 1844, many Americans had already witnessed women's writing in periodicals, but this work appeared almost exclusively in magazines that reinforced feminine "place" in terms of domesticity and morality, one of the most famous examples being Sarah Josepha Hale's *Godey's Lady's Book*, established in 1830.[3] Female writers and their readers were customarily constrained to themes of literary domesticity and, in particular, to the language of sentimentality pervading the antebellum marketplace. Fuller, however, not only worked in a male-dominated venue, the daily urban newspaper, she also reported on asylums and prisons and the conditions affecting madwomen and female inmates. Writing about public institutions, she was one of the first newspaper women to position female rhetoric strategically and to pen forceful articles within the masculinized space of the mass-market newspaper. In amplifying her sympathetic voice, she redirected conversations about women, work, and sympathy.[4]

Most Americans in the 1840s would have been surprised to learn that a woman worked—and drew a full-time salary—for a paper as prominent as Greeley's *Tribune,* and while newspapers rarely used bylines, Greeley did what he could to foreground Fuller's identity by printing an asterisk or "star" at the conclusion of Fuller's columns to highlight their novelty.[5] She became, literally, the star of the *Tribune.* Although most readers likely did not realize that the columns were composed by a woman (one letter to the editor, for instance, praised the author's "good and manly independence"), other readers were in the know—and they were not necessarily happy about the prospect of a woman speaking so directly through the pages of a major New York paper.[6] An article in the *Courier and Enquirer,* for instance, criticized Fuller for writing "so foolishly, and with so much vanity" about issues that "requir[e] something more" than her supposedly superficial knowledge (in this case knowledge about the death penalty). The subtext is clear; presumably only a man would have knowledge about—or should contribute to—public debates about crime and punishment. Fuller attacked this presumption head on: "We were not aware that the Bible, or the welfare of human beings were subjects improper for the consideration of 'females,' whether '*fair*' or otherwise. We had also supposed that, in the field of literature, the meeting was not between man and woman, but between mind and mind."[7]

The attention to Fuller's gender foregrounds the peculiarity of her position as a paid employee for a mass-market daily. In writing for a New York paper, she blurred the ideological binary of private and public, nurtured her growing sensibility of social sympathy, and encouraged the use of emotionality to instruct a public already well versed in the language of sentimentality. Fuller correctly assumed a readership significantly larger than that for her earlier work. She hoped in *Woman in the Nineteenth Century,* for instance, that perhaps "a few" of her words to American women "may not be addressed in vain. One here and there may listen."[8] But the *Dial*—the transcendentalist periodical Fuller had edited earlier in the 1840s—boasted a circulation of only three hundred. An urban newspaper, in contrast, provided a medium through which she could reach a large audience; the 1844 *Tribune* boasted an estimated circulation of thirty thousand.[9] Fuller understood that no other platform afforded a comparable opportunity to convey her message. Within the pages of a newspaper, Fuller could model a sympathetic ideology that simultaneously established her own public, professional authority.

After contextualizing the *New-York Tribune* within the antebellum periodical marketplace, this chapter examines how Fuller's use of sympathy, which emerges most noticeably in her writings on prisons and insane asylums, functioned "to speak effectually some right words to a large circle," as she wrote a friend in 1844.[10] In validating her feminine voice, Fuller produced a reportage that channeled sympathy to make her own previously private voice public, within the context of a predominantly masculine profession.

Laying the Groundwork: Fuller's "Private" Life

Born in 1810 in Cambridgeport, Massachusetts, to Timothy and Margarett Crane Fuller, Sarah Margaret Fuller, the eldest of nine children, grew up in an intensely intellectual home. Pushed by a demanding and authoritarian father, Fuller devoured her family's considerable library as a child. But precociousness came at a price—the adult Fuller characterized herself as a "bright and ugly" child.[11] Her lack of exposure to children outside her own family possibly hindered social development, and her only formal education came through two years at Prescott Seminary for Young Ladies in Groton, Massachusetts. Fuller's life, though, took a dramatic turn when she met Ralph Waldo Emerson in 1836 and began a somewhat tumultuous relationship with the American Scholar, which lasted until her drowning death in 1850.

Although critics frequently emphasize the intense privacy that marked Fuller's early intellectual life, Charles Capper and others point out that she progressed steadily toward a more public persona, which culminated in her position with the *New-York Tribune*. As early as 1839, she was experimenting with how to broadcast her ideas to an ever-widening circle of listeners and readers. Fuller's Boston Conversations, for example, which ran from 1839 to 1844, let her lead women through debates on religion, literature, and philosophy. These parlor talks served as "an innovative and socially accept-able alternative to the public lecture platform," a "transitional site between private, social writing and . . . public, professional writing."[12] Through the experience, Fuller learned to craft her arguments to appeal to a more diverse audience, setting the stage for her later work at the *New-York Tribune*.

Fuller also progressed toward her role at the *Tribune* through exposure to another segment of the American periodical marketplace through the *Dial* (1840–44), a quarterly "utterance of a small fraternity of scholars and thinkers" initially edited by Fuller—and widely pilloried by critics.[13] Her most significant work for that journal was the essay "The Great Lawsuit, Man Versus Men, Woman versus Women," later expanded into the seminal *Woman in the Nineteenth Century*. The *Dial* essay and the resulting book, a "foundational text for the women's rights movement in America," were Fuller's first attempts to challenge publicly the ideological boundaries between sexes and to assert her right as a woman to move beyond a con-stricted domestic sphere.[14] Horace Greeley, whose publishing firm brought out *Woman in the Nineteenth Century* in February 1845, proclaimed it "the loftiest and most commanding assertion yet made of the right of woman to be regarded and treated as an independent, intelligent, rational being, entitled to an equal voice in framing and modifying the laws she is required to obey, and controlling and disposing of the property she has inherited or aided to acquire."[15]

Greeley's words suggest the political and professional import of Fuller's book, and her early experiences laid the groundwork for the remarkable position she would hold as a reporter for the *New-York Tribune*. Her shift from a "private" speaker and author within the confines of American tran-scendentalist circles to a public identity reflected her own refashioning of

Emersonian philosophies about self-culture into a belief in self-culture as tied to public, reform-based acts. Indeed, Fuller's move to New York arose within the context of discussions about the role transcendentalism should play in social reform. Emerson, for one, advocated studied introspection over broad-scale change and even denigrated the "demon of reform," claiming progressive movements only led to "superficial skirmishes, a reshuffling of the cards."[16] Indeed, the philosopher frequently displayed a "patrician dislike of reformers" and an "intense dislike of all forms of association."[17] Privileging the potential of individual over cultural perfection, Emerson characterized collective efforts as secondary to self-reliance and self-reform, though other prominent transcendentalists, among them Orestes Brownson and George Ripley, advocated social advancement and a more active approach to the alleviation of cultural ills, including gender inequality and prison and asylum reform.

Fuller herself, by the early 1840s, sought to meld the process of individual, private transformation with that of public transformation, and to project the voice of "self culture" to a wide audience.[18] Where she had once "env[ied] those who had kept within the protecting bound of private life," she wrote in 1840, "I will not."[19] Fuller's "inward life," as Jeffrey Steele argues, "was evolving into new expressive forms that eventually linked passionate commitment to public questions of urban reform," particularly in prisons and asylums.[20] While in New York, she finally solidified and expanded her belief in individual reform into advocacy for broader social change. If she had been previously concerned primarily with the question of individual progress, in the city she attempted to translate those philosophies for a mass readership rather than for a coterie of like-minded individuals, and in her readings of public institutions, the literary rhetoric of sympathy guided her movement into a professional role.

GREELEY'S *NEW-YORK TRIBUNE* AND SYMPATHETIC REPORTAGE

Of all American newspaper editors in the 1840s, Horace Greeley was the most likely to take the radical step of hiring a woman as a permanent staff member. While Greeley was destined to become one of the most influential editors in nineteenth-century American journalism, the *New-York Tribune* to which Fuller came in 1844 was still in its fledgling years, having opened its doors on Ann Street only three years earlier before moving to Nassau Street after an 1845 fire destroyed the paper's original building. With a professional staff of only four people in 1844—a commercial editor, a literary editor, and two local reporters, plus numerous place-rate correspondents—the *Tribune*'s circulation soon made it New York's third largest paper.[21] Greeley situated his newspaper carefully against the clamoring pages of the 1830s and 1840s urban penny press. Unlike traditional papers, which typically sold for six cents and concentrated on economic and political news, penny papers were accessible virtually to everyone. They introduced into the newspaper business an element of sensationalism that would dominate the marketplace until the end of the nineteenth century (and that, of course, played an important role in how Nellie Bly and Elizabeth Jordan framed their own conceptions of sympathy). Driven by emerging print technologies, dramatically increasing urban population, rising adult literacy rates, and an explicit interest in "the common man," penny papers spoke to a mass readership that spanned social classes. These papers marketed themselves not as political party organs for the privileged few, as did traditional papers, but as egalitarian and independent publications, free from overt political influence. They fueled an incredible increase in the number of antebellum newspapers and were made possible by a voracious audience.

Benjamin Day's *New York Sun*, established in 1833, was the first paper to deploy a formula that would soon characterize the penny press—a combination of crime reporting, purple prose, and sheer sensationalism. Day proclaimed on September 3, 1833, in his inaugural edition, that he would "lay before the public, at a price within the means of everyone, all the news of the day." And he meant *all* the news, whether true or not. Readers reveled in police reports, human-interest stories, and tales of remarkable discoveries (including the famous "Moon Hoax," through which readers of the *Sun* were led to believe that humanoid life had been spotted on the moon). The formula worked, spectacularly so. Within just two years, circulation at the *Sun* rose from five thousand to fifteen thousand copies a day.[22] Other topics, such as the Mary Rogers murder (which Edgar Allan Poe fictionalized in his story "The Mystery of Marie Rogêt") and the murder of prostitute Helen Jewett, exponentially grew the audience for penny papers.[23] Enormous profits followed, as did numerous competing publications, including, most famously and contentiously, James Gordon Bennett's *New York Herald*, which "weav[ed] together a coarse canvas of sensational murders, railroad accidents, and steamboat explosions along with unlimited promotion of merchandise," leading to "gory and grotesque sheets" that "stood on the threshold where public and private merged, where orality and print coexisted."[24] Penny papers made private lives and private agonies public, ripe for titillating, melodramatic, and voyeuristic consumption by a hungry audience. This self-serving consumption of news was, additionally, the journalism against which Fuller ultimately labored.

In 1841 Greeley entered this crowded and competitive New York periodical marketplace. The number of newspaper titles had grown threefold since the first penny papers appeared, and the editor sought his own publishing niche. Greeley admired the egalitarian spirit of the penny press, but, though his own paper also cost just one cent, he felt uncomfortable with his rivals' overly dramatic reportage. He created instead an affordable yet refined alternative within the periodical marketplace, although the *Tribune* offered its own share of sensational stories in its four pages. Such attention-grabbing headlines as "Outrageous Assault upon an Old Man," "Sentence of Death," and "Steamboat Collision and Loss of Life" abound, but Greeley's articles were subdued in comparison with the florid style of other penny papers. Further differentiating the paper, Greeley aligned the *Tribune* with the Whigs, whereas competing papers in New York trumpeted their alleged non-partisanship. Greeley, however, a man of contradictions throughout his career, refused to toe the party line exclusively. According to descriptions by his biographers, he was a "Jeffersonian democrat who belonged to the conservative Whig party, a social reformer who upheld the high tariff, a man of peace who strongly supported wartime conscription, a man of the city who loved farming."[25] He envisioned the *Tribune* as "a journal removed alike from servile partisanship on the one hand and from gagged mincing neutrality on the other."[26]

Greeley also attended readily to reform issues, seeking, as he later remarked, "to advance the interests of the people, and to promote their Moral, Political and Social well-being."[27] Indeed, Greeley's own keen sense of democracy and thirst for social change essentially drove editorial practices at the *Tribune*. Dedicated to a number of cases throughout his life—including Fourierism, abolitionism, pacifism, and temperance—he committed himself above all else to the elevation of the masses. Under this mantra, Greeley challenged the fare of more sensational penny papers, focusing instead on the arts, moral issues, and reform. It was to prove a productive fit for Fuller and her own developing sense of a gendered, sympathetic public voice.

Greeley had long admired her work before he hired Fuller to write columns for his paper in the summer of 1844. He had lingered on the periphery of transcendentalist circles, drawn by discussions about the paradoxical relationship between individual and community and the idealized picture of "man thinking," a phrase that could describe the editor himself. In 1844, Greeley visited Brook Farm and promoted the publication of Fuller's *Summer on the Lakes,* and his wife, Mary Greeley, participated in Fuller's Boston Conversations. Moreover, he appreciated Fuller's work in the *Dial* and encouraged her to expand "The Great Lawsuit" into *Woman in the Nineteenth Century,* which coincided with the beginning of her *Tribune* position. Though hiring a woman on salary was an unprecedented act for a New York editor, Greeley boasted a commitment to women's rights in the workplace and equitable pay between the sexes.

As part of the *Tribune* contract, Greeley asked Fuller to write two or three columns per week, and by all accounts she embraced the opportunity, recognizing her unique capacity to address a massive new audience, far beyond the confines of an intimate Boston parlor. Anticipating her move to the city, she wrote friend Maria Rotch in September 1844, "It is a position that offers many advantages and may be turned to much good."[28] Later that year, as she settled into her job, she assured Samuel Ward that her work "is so central, and affords a far more various view of life than any I ever before was in."[29] The variety came from the city itself, with "the bracing concreteness of its problems," which, Bell Gale Chevigny contends, encouraged her "own growing mastery and complete freedom of action, her vast audience and their responsiveness."[30] New York in the 1840s, locus of massive population shifts, new industrialism, and urban crowding, became a space in which residents could craft identities, where neat boundaries between social classes and genders begged to be tested.[31] Ignoring friends who objected that the role of newspaper woman did not suit her, Fuller insisted on the importance of her work and her desire to speak to a broad audience. Emerson, to cite one example, sighed that Fuller had given up genuine literary calling in favor of the journalistic "treadmill."[32] Fuller, however, had no patience for such criticism. They "think I ought to produce something excellent," she protested, "while I am satisfied to aid in the great work of popular education."[33] While a great deal of that work involved writing literary criticism and art reviews, Fuller devoted a fair share of her 250 columns to an exploration of the city's social issues. As a reviewer, she commented on literature and the arts, but she also contemplated class division, surveyed benevolent institutions, and attempted to forge sympathetic bonds between the readers and subjects of her reports. And the city itself—as fashioned through the pages of one of its flagship newspapers—offered Fuller a public stage for commentary about these very issues.

INSTITUTIONALIZED WOMEN, SYMPATHY, AND THE PUBLIC/PRIVATE DIVIDE

Urged forward by his dedication to social improvement, Greeley encouraged his unusual new employee to report on New York's institutions, including asylums and prisons. Fuller was already acquainted with reformers like William Henry Channing, who was president of the New York Prison Association; Lydia Maria Child, who, as I discuss in chapter 1, published her own articles about American prison conditions; Georgiana Bruce, assistant warden of women prisoners at New York's Sing Sing prison, whom Fuller had met at Brook Farm; and Quaker activist Isaac Hopper and his daughter Abigail. In fact, shortly before she assumed her *Tribune* post, Fuller visited Sing Sing, accompanied by Channing and Caroline Sturgis. Eliza Farnham, who in 1844 was appointed superintendent of America's "first purpose-built women's prison," had initiated a bold program of rehabilitation for inmates.[34] It was a position she earned, in part, through Greeley's reformist connections. Convinced of the need for humane, gentle treatment and dedicated programs for rehabilitation, Farnham introduced such therapeutic comforts as reading to the inmates, allowing conversation between the prisoners, and providing flowers to well-behaved women— changes consonant with the philosophies of moral treatment practiced in many asylums and prisons in the 1830s and 1840s.[35]

At Farnham's invitation, Fuller visited Sing Sing in October 1844 and returned on Christmas Day to meet personally with incarcerated women. She followed this visit with tours of other institutions between January and March 1845, gathering impressions for her reportage and furthering her own sense of a sympathy-laden transcendentalism designed for the public sphere. The articles Fuller produced about the Bloomingdale Insane Asylum, the Tombs prison, and Blackwell's Island, as well as her favorable report on Sing Sing, reveal a woman fully immersed in the culture of these institutions and the problem of how best to represent them to the reading public, and how to do so without being dismissed because of her gender. Her articles became a way to immerse her audience in the realities of incarceration.

Fuller's reports on prison and asylum conditions dovetail with the journalistic and fictional offerings I survey in the previous chapter, including ones published in the *New-York Tribune*.[36] The December 20, 1844, edition of Greeley's paper, for example, includes a prison reform piece penned by Lydia Maria Child.[37] Similarly, Fuller's article on a home for "discharged female convicts" immediately precedes "Bridge of Sighs," a poem by Thomas Hood concerning a deceased prostitute—the "star" that symbolizes Fuller's authorship literally and figuratively introduces the poem, which calls for the reader not to "treat" the dead woman "scornfully," but to

> Think of her mournfully,
> Greatly, and humanly:
> Not of the stains of her
> All that remains of her
> Now is pure womanly.[38]

Another article, "Trip from Cincinnati to Cleveland and Detroit," contrasts the beauty of a prison's grounds with the suffering within, urging readers to weep for the prisoners and calling for public enactment of a sympathetic ethos.

For her part, Fuller published work in this genre concerning the Bloomingdale Asylum for the Insane, where Superintendent Pliny Earle's "refined sympathies and intellectual discernment" had "appl[ied] the best" moral treatment available. The asylum, she notes with approval, "is conducted on the most wise and liberal plan known at the present day," a "house of refuge where those too deeply wounded or disturbed in body or spirit to keep up that semblance or degree of sanity" required by daily life "may be soothed by gentle care" and "intelligent sympathy."[39] These "unfortunates" receive gentle, heart-felt treatment, while "half a century ago" they "would have been chained in solitary cells, screaming out their anguish till silenced by threats or blows, lost, forsaken, hopeless, a blight to earth, a libel against heaven."[40] Fuller's praise of sympathetic treatment is perhaps most obvious in her description of the Valentine's Day dance at Bloomingdale, especially in comparison to the comparatively mocking articles about asylum dances outlined in chapter 1. The patients "were well-dressed, in care and taste," and "the dancing was better than" one might observe at a dance for sane people "because there was less of affectation and ennui." One patient who captures Fuller's attention is a "blue-stocking lady," whose "'highly intellectual' vivacity, expressed no less in her headdress than her manner, was just that touch above the common with which the illustrator of Dickens has thought fit to heighten the charms of Mrs. Leo Hunter" of *The Pickwick Papers*. The whole dance is "done decently, and in order," and any "slight symptoms of impatience here and there were easily soothed by the approach" of the gentle Dr. Earle, "the touch of whose hand seemed to possess a talismanic power to soothe." The dance's participants are virtually indistinguishable from her own friends and acquaintances, Fuller implies, or yours, reader. Gone are the condescending amusements prevalent in other, predominantly male-authored descriptions of asylum dances in contemporary articles.

The narrative tone in the Bloomingdale article establishes a theme to which Fuller returns repeatedly in her social reporting: the need for both personal and public sympathy, echoing the feminine sympathy on display in her writing. "Our City Charities," to provide another example, sees Fuller touring the Bellevue Alms House, Farm School, and Insane Asylum and Blackwell's Island. Echoing other asylum visit pieces, this article opens with a careful bit of gothic scene setting as Fuller describes the day's dark, rainy outlook: "The aspect of Nature was sad; what is worse, it was dull and dubious.... The sky was leaden and lowering, the air unkind and piercing." In literary fashion, Fuller uses her storytelling abilities to evoke desired responses; she creates a mood before she opens institutional doors for her readers. While other journalists, in contrast, might extend the gothic setting to a survey of the monsters lurking within the building, Fuller urges *Tribune* readers beyond the forbidding exteriors of these institutions and asks them to forgo the stereotyped narrative framing, peering instead at the conditions inside (with its literal madwomen in the attic) until the "heart of the community" can be awakened "to do what is right." Fuller rejects the superficial gaze that turns asylum patients into two-dimensional figures of pity, scorn, or amusement. For the idealist Fuller, looking deeply into the heart of the institution—making the condition of institutionalized people evident through her own words—will prompt readers to aid "their fellow-creatures in any way, public or private."[41] In exposing the institutional space, the mediating writer evokes sympathy and prods newspaper readers to exercise the "right principles" necessary for improved conditions within the institutions.

As she guides readers through the alms house, the farm school, and the asylum, Fuller models "right principles" by gazing sympathetically on such potentially carnivalesque figures as a young Dutch dwarf abandoned by a circus keeper—a figure who "would have suggested a thousand poetical images and fictions to the mind of Victor Hugo or Sir Walter Scott"—and a Catholic novitiate who continually chants her mass, "her face attenuated and very pallid, her eyes large, open, fixed and bright with a still fire." Fuller again constructs an almost novelistic portrait of her subjects, yet she disrupts her audience's implicit urge to view the insane in either dismissive or degrading terms.[42] In asking readers to envision the Bellevue patients as they would characters in a novel, she insists, somewhat paradoxically, that they read this true tale read more deeply than they would a novel's pages. The dwarf and the Catholic novitiate are not, finally, mere fictions in a novel that can be set aside, not literary characters for which a reader might experience only fleeting sympathy. Rather, Fuller pushes her audience to "read" the institutional unfortunates so carefully that to read her article is to enter physically into the institution, softening all boundaries between subject, writer, and reader.

If Fuller paints a vivid picture of women in the asylum, the penitentiary and the spectacle of the imprisoned female body interest her even more. She had "always felt great interest in [fallen women], who are trampled in the mud to gratify the brute appetites of men," she wrote Maria Rotch in January 1845.[43] Still, what Fuller sees during her visit to the prison on Blackwell's Island startles her, especially in contrast to conditions at Sing Sing, where she witnessed moral treatment in action. The city penitentiary seems devoid of sympathy—it is a place of "barbarity" and brutality, a model of discipline rather than reform of prisoners. In essence, it rejects the belief in inherent human worth, central to transcendentalist philosophy. Without efforts to rehabilitate prisoners built on models of sympathy, Fuller asks, where are the "good influences and steady aim to raise" the fallen "from the pit of infamy and wo into which they have fallen?"[44] As Steele notes, Fuller, akin to other reformers, "suggests that the cause of reform can be advanced only by basing it upon the expression of sympathetic feeling," expression that was already a mainstay of contemporary sentimental novels and of Farnham's reforms at Sing Sing, in Fuller's judgment.[45] The prison on Blackwell's Island, in contrast, lacks "that more righteous feeling" of sympathy for the prisoner, the only quality that can yield lasting reform.[46] Fuller here envisions social transformation made possible by increased public financial support as well as charitable contributions from private individuals, the group she targets with her sympathetic appeals.

Two months later, Fuller confronted the issue of housing for "discharged female convicts" in an article that draws even more directly on a rhetoric of sympathy and sketches direct parallels between the sympathy readers extend to fictional characters and the sympathy they should extend instead to the residents of New York's prisons and asylums. "Asylum for Discharged Female Convicts" describes a shelter recently established by "the ladies of the Prison Association," a halfway house that lacks sufficient food, furniture, clothing, and books. Beseeching her audience to aid the female "convicts"—code language for prostitutes—Fuller asserts that the poor among her readers will already "know how to sympathize with those who are not only poor but degraded, diseased, likely to be harried onward to a shameful, hopeless death." Lacking this natural sympathy, more fortunate readers must develop other ways to "feel for those who have not been guarded either by social influence or inward strength from that first mistake which the opinion of the world makes irrevocable for women alone." Fuller targets wealthier readers, who, she fears, may lack human sympathy because the comforts of their class have allowed them to sink into a state of "ennui, dejection, and a gradual ossification." A moral crevasse yawns between privileged readers and the unfortunate subjects of Fuller's story. But visiting the asylum for fallen women, even in print, awakens "a thoughtful, sympathetic, and beneficent existence," something akin to the sympathy that well-drawn literary characters might evoke.[47] In essence, Fuller hopes to act as midwife for a sympathy born out of her own reportage: the act of reading the article will awaken an active sympathy that will stretch far beyond the edges of the newsprint.

Fuller's praise for a *home* for fallen women is particularly evocative. American fiction in the early and mid-nineteenth century witnessed "a preoccupation with familial feeling as the foundation for sympathy, and sympathy as the basis of a democratic republic."[48] However, where many critics have described sentimentality's focus on domesticity within the boundaries of biological relationships, sentimental literature forced open those boundaries and articulated instead a redefinition of family, one based on sympathetic bonds that might supersede biological lines. Fuller cultivates that sympathetic preoccupation as she envisions the "asylum for discharged female convicts" as a place where outcast women, in concert with their benefactors, will craft a family based on the shared "biology" of feeling. The article transforms the private home into a public one, in essence opening the four walls of the traditional domestic space so readers can protect the most vulnerable and misunderstood members of the "family." The author, herself a public figure, serves as the mediator who brings this family together through her journalistic lens.

In pleading for support of this home, Fuller envisions a reader who will act as an "angel" in "a stranger's form" and aid needy women. Though Fuller cannot approach these angels—her readers—in person, she can rouse their sympathies through the pages of the *New-York Tribune:*

> We cannot go to those still and sheltered homes and tell [readers] the tales that would be sure to awaken the heart to a deep and active interest in this matter. But should these words meet their eyes we would say, Have you entertained your leisure hours with the Mysteries of Paris or the pathetic story of Violet Woodville? Then you have some idea how innocence worthy of the brightest planet may be betrayed by want, or by the most generous tenderness; how the energies of a noble reformation may lie hidden beneath the ashes of a long burning.[49]

Recalling the titles of two contemporary novels about fallen women, Marian Dora Malet's 1836 *Violet Woodville; or, the Life of an Opera Dancer* and Eugene Sue's 1843 best-selling *Les Mystères de Paris,* Fuller links sympathy-laden novels to the city's realism. Fuller's references resonate within the context of more sensationalized, cheap novels and broadsides about seduction and prostitution that constituted a significant portion of the literary marketplace in the 1830s and 1840s.[50] Sue's fiction, in particular, receives Fuller's approval: in some of her literary reviews for the *Tribune,* she applauds the novelist's use of emotion to champion a message of reform.

In one column, she praises Sue's conviction that literature can make "the heart of mankind . . . beat with one great hope, one love," so that "his tales of horror" might not become actual "tragedies."[51] The novel she references in her article on "discharged female convicts," *The Mysteries of Paris,* is a city-mystery novel, meant to highlight the sinister underbelly of urban life with an eye toward mass reform. As I suggest in chapter 1, these fictions sometimes hid behind the finest veneer of reform and were composed in "voyeur style," an "indulgently participatory rhetoric that reveled in titillating description of debauchery and seduction."[52] Although city-mystery novels ostensibly intended to improve conditions for the less fortunate, readers may have been more likely to consume the sensation of the text alone, reading in a detached fashion and ignoring meatier political agendas.

Fuller sidesteps a parallel pitfall in her own writing by narrating her own exposé. She urges readers to "link these fictions, which have made you weep, with facts around you where your pity might be of use." She transforms, that is, the private act of novel reading and the sympathy readers expend on literary creations, into a public act of sympathy—a *useful* sympathy. Fuller characterizes fiction reading as a luxury, a pointless exercise of pity for characters that exist only in the imagination. The characters she draws in her own writing, in contrast, would actually benefit from the reader's tears. Use what you've learned from your reading, she urges the newspaper audience: sympathy for outcast women in fiction is ultimately wasted unless applied toward its ideal social end. Fuller's exhortations grow more pointed as she commands her readers: "Go to the penitentiary at Blackwell's Island," "see" the inmates with their "sad ruins of past loveliness," "see [the] little girls huddled in a corner," and finally "think what 'sweet seventeen' was to you, and what it is to them, and see if you do not wish to aid in any enterprise that gives them a chance of better days."[53] Compelling readers to sympathize actively with marginalized women, Fuller transforms sympathy from a private, novelistic, leisure enterprise into an immediate social act within the context of New York's institutions.

Fuller's fictional references are anything but random. She understood the appeal of popular literature, but, perhaps because of popularity itself, she generally held such novels in low regard—she once referred to popular novelists, for instance, as "female scribblers" who contributed "the paltriest of offspring of the human brain."[54] Still, Fuller's work in the city alerted her to the political and professional potential of novel-reading. Reading the journalism strictly in opposition to popular fiction bypasses Fuller's careful rhetorical appropriation. Rather than reject popular literature outright, she adopts its emotional conventions, outfits it with her own sensibility, and capitalizes on her readership's tastes, redirecting attention toward reform in the process. Fuller, that is, repackages a mode of writing primarily associated with female sentimental fiction and sells it in a medium primarily associated with men—the newspaper—and reinforces her own journalistic voice in the process.

Fuller, however, anticipates the possibly negative reaction to this public, female voice. Her 1846 article "Prison Discipline," for instance—a survey of four prison and asylum annual reports—equates sympathy for asylum and prison inmates with "the divine love of Jesus, who redoubled his encouragements to the prodigal son instead of punishing him for past transgressions." Recognizing the somewhat mawkish nature of her parallel, she heads off resisting readers: "Harsh bigots may sneer at this spirit of mercy as 'sickly sentimentality,' but the spark has been struck, and, nothing daunted, the fire glows, grows, rises, and begins to cast a light around."[55] Fuller reads and reviews the four annual reports in the same way she reads and reviews books for the *Tribune*. Her deep involvement with cultures of fiction, as displayed in her book reviews, spirals outward in all of her prison and asylum articles so that sympathetic reading transcends the bounds of private and public, regardless of her own—or her reader's—sex. In essence, she democratizes reading and holds a conversation based on sympathy between the consumer and the subject of the text, ultimately blurring the line between spectator and spectacle. And the woman's newspaper voice is the vehicle facilitating that conversation. As Bean and Myerson point out, the *Tribune* articles expose an "increased understanding of the opportunities for political action open to women" and "her own role in shaping them through one of the most popular newspapers of the day." For Fuller, writing becomes a way of asserting her political and public identity at a time when critics of transcendentalism accused it of ignoring actual reform in favor of theoretical contemplation of cultural inadequacies. What emerges in Fuller's asylum and prison articles, then, is "an integration of theory with practice," an attempt to translate the diverse philosophies of transcendentalism into programs for action and reform, based on a model in which the private act of reading becomes public and the bodies of institutionalized women likewise become public through the mediating lens of the sympathetic female reporter.[56] Emerson's "transparent eyeball" gains a body on the pages of a New York newspaper.

Fuller's insistence on public sympathy found its way into her revision of "The Great Lawsuit" for Horace Greeley. In *Woman in the Nineteenth Century,* she refers to her prison visits and argues that the incarcerated prostitutes had sold their bodies in desperate bids to obtain the trappings of luxury in which more fortunate women—presumably among Fuller's female readers themselves—indulge. "Now I ask you, my sisters," Fuller admonishes, "if the women at the fashionable house be not answerable for those women being in the prison?" Gaze not on the prostitute's ruined body, she insists; turn your lens inward as well. Consider your own culpability, and public reform will more likely follow: "I would urge upon those women who have not yet considered this subject, to do so. Do not forget the unfortunates who dare not cross your guarded way. If it do not suit you to act with those who have organized measures of reform, then hold not yourself excused from acting in private. Seek out these degraded women, give them tender sympathy, counsel, employment. Take the place of mothers, such as might have saved them originally."[57] As in her newspaper articles, Fuller issues forceful, direct commands, urging her readers to action: "hold yourself" accountable, "seek out" the unfortunate, "take" your place in the family engendered by sympathy. In a rhetoric that verges on sermonology, she compels readers to act publicly, even as she acts in public herself.

If Fuller's article on the home for discharged female convicts envisions a new kind of domestic space, she more explicitly revises the definitions of family by asking readers to "take the place of mothers." Yet, in making the prostitutes' bodies public for the reader, Fuller metaphorically sells them to her readership, and she risks transforming the act of sympathy into a voyeuristic indulgence. Institutionalized and incarcerated bodies were already sold in the marketplace of 1840s asylum and prison tourism, and Fuller seems keenly aware that the process of gazing upon unfortunate women edges uncomfortably close to consuming another person's suffering unreflectively and uncritically, thereby deriving entertainment from it, a point she addresses directly in her assessment of the Bellevue Alms House. Describing "mothers with their newborn infants" exposed to the "gaze of the stranger," she acknowledges that the residents of the alms house doubtless "dislike the scrutiny of strangers."[58] Fuller places herself in the role of the stranger, the visiting spectator who surveys the specter of poverty firsthand. However, she compels readers not only to contemplate the impoverished new mothers but to view, as well, the reporter as she looks upon these women. The article acts, that is, as a metanarrative about spectacle, in which consumers of the text, if they are genuinely sympathetic readers, refuse the temptation to distance themselves from the subject of the story and instead scrutinize their own commitment to fellow feeling. Readers must, in some sense, see through the reporter's eyes even as the reporter attempts to see through the mother's eyes. Fuller renders the mothers' private pain public, but she does not report coldly or sensationalistically. Rather, she characterizes herself within the text to create a genuine sympathetic bond that transgresses boundaries between private reader and publicized mother. Writing in the context of extremely profitable penny press sensationalism, then, Fuller turns the spectacle of sensation on its head. Where contemporary newspapers frequently depicted incarceration and insanity with detached voyeurism, Fuller insists on sympathetic identification. She transforms the gaze on the other into a gaze inward, a form of observation that moves from private reflection to public sympathy and to reform, directed through the professional voice of the female.

Fuller's references to fiction and the connection between fictional sympathy and reform highlight the gendered edge of the medium in which they appear. If convention held that the newspaper was, in professional terms if not in actual readership, a masculine space, as a newspaper woman, Fuller situates herself in a socially unstable position. She speaks in a "masculine" forum, the front page of the newspaper, about social problems that are, at least according to privileged cultural ideologies, not readily within her realm of influence. Her decision to deploy the language of sympathy and her allusions to popular, sentimental novels function as rhetorically savvy attempts to close the gap between public and private, male and female, fiction-reading and newspaper-writing, all under the mantle of "feeling right," as Harriet Beecher Stowe would phrase it.[59] By deploying this language, Fuller connects her potentially radical call for sympathy toward institutionalized citizens with the less threatening, gendered language of the broader literary marketplace.

In August 1846, Fuller left New York for Europe, embarking on a new career journey—that of foreign correspondent for the *Tribune,* a position for which she penned thirty-seven dispatches, many concerning the Italian

Risorgimento movement.[60] In these pieces, Fuller continued to ask her readers to travel with her from reading to action, and her "tactic for cata-lyzing social activism" in the Italian dispatches also continued "to target the individual reader," a narrative strategy she perfected as an urban newspaper woman.[61] It was in New York, after all, that she honed her public voice and learned the power of sympathy in terms of woman's professionalism and the "networks of love and sympathy that might be constructed in the public sphere."[62] Midway through her tenure in the city, Fuller wrote her brother Richard, "I have now a position where if I can devot [*sic*] myself entirely to use its occasions, a noble career is before me yet. . . . I want that my friends should *wish* me now to act in my public career rather than towards them personally. I have given almost all my young energies to personal relations. I no longer feel inclined to do this, and wish to share and impel the general stream of thought."[63] As this letter suggests, Fuller was fascinated by the size of her potential readership, a sentiment she echoed in correspondence to her brother Eugene: "The public part . . . is entirely satisfying. . . . I am truly interested in this great field which opens before me and it is pleasant to be sure of a chance at a half a hundred thousand readers."[64] If some of her friends in transcendentalist circles belittled the mass audience that she admired, the writer reveled in the phenomenon of publicity and, more directly, in its potential social usefulness.

Fuller's remarks to her brothers showcase her own sensibilities and her un-derstanding that her position as a newspaper woman had provided an unpar-alleled chance to dismantle artificial boundaries between public and private, male and female. While she realized she could not directly and immediately alleviate conditions in prisons, asylums, and other institutions—let alone open wide the doors of newspaper journalism to other women who yearned to do the same—she nevertheless empowered the "degree of sympathetic response" that arose from her writing.[65] In New York, Fuller also developed a keener sense of her own audience and learned to reach readers in a way that both encouraged and challenged them. At a time when she was broadening her earlier emphasis on self-culture to encompass a more muscular advocacy of reform, Fuller was also aware that as a front-page journalist she must be strategic in how she framed her reporting. The language of sympathy allowed her to craft a space in which she could speak as a woman with authority.

CHAPTER 3

Entering Unceremoniously
Fanny Fern, Sympathy, and Tales of Confinement

*[Happiness] is to look round an editorial sanctum, inwardly chuckling at the
forlorn appearance it makes without feminine fingers to keep it tidy.*

—Fanny Fern, *Fern Leaves from Fanny's Portfolio,* second series

In 1872, world-famous newspaper columnist Fanny Fern reflected on a
suffrage meeting she had recently attended, marking with appreciation the
eloquent speeches men delivered in support of women's rights. However,
some other women attending the meeting diverted her attention: "At the
reporters' table sat two young lady reporters side by side with the breth-
ren of the same class. Truly, remarked I to my companion, it is very well
to plead for women's rights, but more delicious to me is the sight of those
two girls *taking them.*"[1] What Fern observed was an example of the small
but growing collection of newspaper women employed after the Civil War,
professional positions available in no small part because of women like
Fern herself, who had written for the papers since 1851. In the twilight of
her career, she could celebrate the progress women had made in securing
seats at the reporters' table.

Twenty years earlier, those seats were not open, and Fern, as an
early-generation newspaper woman, had "take[n] them" for herself by
deploying the rhetorical weapons readily available to her, including the
language of sympathy. In her most popular novel, *Ruth Hall,* Fern figures
journalism as a "site of gender discipline, where her legitimacy as a journalist always is in question" by men.[2] The question of legitimacy was central
to Fern in her newspaper writing, as well. She reflected repeatedly on the

problem of gender and professionalism as she wrote for one of the most popular mass-market papers of the nineteenth century, the *New York Ledger,* which boasted a circulation of some four hundred thousand subscribers, owing in no small part to the quality and appeal of Fern's writing.[3] Though she is best known for her sharp, satirical writing about women's issues, sentimentality was also one of her favored styles, and she tied her journalistic pictures of domesticity to a public sensibility by penning forceful articles about serious issues, including prison and asylum reform. In her articles, Fern offered a blend of frank realism and sentimental prose and appropriated sympathetic discourse to underscore her authority as a newspaper woman.[4] These rhetorical choices showcase the confidence she took in her own voice and her conviction that she had the right to speak about a range of public issues within a print medium that was not always eager to listen. In her words about prisons and asylums, in particular, sympathy serves as the chain that links her, as a professional writer, with her large newspaper audience, whom she tutors in the lessons of fellow feeling as she guides readers around America's public institutions. In both her newspaper work and her fiction, she enters the lives of prisoners and madwomen and rejects the casual gaze that dehumanizes them. She models instead the sympathy that marked her, a newspaper woman, as an authoritative commentator on public life.

RAGS TO RICHES, CLAIMS TO FAME

Fern rose to prominence at a time of "seismic ideological shifts regarding work and gender," social changes that lie "at the heart" of her writing.[5] In the 1850s women were learning to fill a newly emergent demand for sentimental, female-authored novels within an expanding literary marketplace. Had it not been for a nearly catastrophic young adulthood, however, Fern's participation in that marketplace might never have occurred. Indeed, her biography veritably echoes the plot of an overwrought sentimental novel. From 1828 to 1829, the teenaged Sara Payson Willis attended Catharine Beecher's school in Hartford, Connecticut, where she distinguished herself by her storytelling and her pranks. At twenty-seven she married Charles Eldredge, and the happy marriage brought three daughters, one of whom died in 1845, the year Charles also died, a victim of typhoid. Pressured by her family, Fern agreed to what would be a disastrous union with Samuel Farrington, whom she left in 1851 after two miserable years. Her bold choice utterly scandalized relatives and friends. When neither her own family nor her first husband's parents would support her and her children after she divorced Farrington, Fern plunged deeper into poverty until, destitute, desperate, and unable to secure any other employment, she was finally able to sell several literary sketches to Boston's *Olive Branch,* a modest weekly newspaper.

The outcome was, to put it mildly, spectacular. From the start, Fern's writing proved an astonishing success; during the two years the *Olive Branch* employed her, the paper saw its circulation rise sharply. Her first column, "The Model Husband," which appeared on June 28, 1851, offers a lighthearted description of a man who readily gives his wife money, cares for the children despite the "soft molasses gingerbread that is rubbed into his hair, coat, and vest," and delays reading his evening newspaper before his beloved "has a chance to run over the advertisements, death, and marriages, etc."[6] The humorous portrait of what women really seek in a mate appealed to readers, and the following day, other Boston papers reprinted the column to great notice, a portent of the popularity Fern would enjoy throughout her career. By September 1851 the *Olive Branch* was printing the byline "Fanny Fern" with her pieces, and readers begged to know, "Who *is* Fanny Fern?" Even Nathaniel Hawthorne (the very week after his infamous diatribe against that "damned mob of scribbling women" who had cornered the popular fiction market) sought the identity of the author who "writes as if the devil was in her," asking his publisher if he could "tell me anything about this Fanny Fern? . . . If you meet her, I wish you would let her know how much I admire her."[7]

Boston's *True Flag* added Fern's writing to its pages in 1852, and she soon branched out to the New York–based *Musical World and Times,* as well. With meteoric speed, Fanny Fern had become a household name, not only in Boston but across the country and in England as more and more papers reprinted her columns. Small wonder. Her frank descriptions of social conditions, parenthood, and gender inequality—to name just three topics—supplied readers with variously sardonic, ironic, and sentimental pictures of life. Indeed, her articles, as biographer Joyce Warren puts it, "sparkle among the dust of convention and artificiality" of much nineteenth-century periodical writing because of their sometimes "brusque tone and candid air." The next year, the publishing house Derby & Miller approached Fern about collecting her work in book form, and *Fern Leaves from Fanny's Portfolio* appeared in June 1853, to great fanfare.[8] Fern's first novel, *Ruth Hall,* soon followed, a thinly disguised roman à clef. However, it was in her "reporting" for Robert Bonner's *New York Ledger,* for which she wrote from 1856 until her death in 1872—never missing a week—that Fern found lasting fame and in the process became the highest-paid newspaper writer in America.

Bonner, an Irish immigrant, learned the craft of newspaper publishing first as a printer's apprentice, then as staff printer in Hartford, Connecticut. Teeming with ambition, he acquired a struggling commercially oriented paper in 1851, which he renamed the *New York Ledger* and relaunched as a periodical "devoted to choice literature, romance, the news, and commerce," as it proclaimed in its masthead (see fig. 5). Bonner carefully balanced his publication between the prurient style of the penny press and the "puritanical morality" of traditionally prim newspapers, printing materials designed to increase the *Ledger*'s popularity among a wide readership, including such diverse items as straight news, poetry, political essays, fiction, and social commentary; that is, the paper blended "public" and "private," the newsy and the literary, male and female interests, all in eight pages per week. This formula worked remarkably well: the *Ledger* increased its circulation from 2,500 to 400,000 subscribers in just nine years, and Fern's contribution to the increase was direct.[9] Within the first year of her employment, circulation had risen to 180,000, higher than that of any other American paper.[10] As with Margaret Fuller and the *New-York Tribune,* the *Ledger* proved an ideal fit for Fern in the development of her professional voice, and, like other journalists, she took interest in public institutions within several of her articles. In keeping with Fuller, however, Fern realized that gender constraints might limit the reach of her voice, and sympathy emerged as a way to exercise her domestic, feminine expertise in order to pass judgment on social and political issues—and the people whose lives were affected by those issues. Modeling sympathetic identification, she immersed herself into these public places, domesticated them, and consequently secured her authoritative position as a newspaper woman.

MODELS OF SYMPATHY

A hallmark of Fern's newspaper writing involved the expression of sympathy for socially marginalized characters, and a survey of how Fern deployed this rhetoric serves as a backdrop for her articles about asylums and pris-

Figure 5. The elaborately engraved masthead of Robert Bonner's *New York Ledger* promised readers "choice literature, romance, the news, and commerce." (Author's collection)

ons, more specifically. The *Olive Branch* article "Mistaken Philanthropy," for example, illustrates how she channeled the power of sympathy even from the early stages of her career. Fern challenges readers of this piece to accept as a family member any "poor wretch" who "comes to you for charity," as if that "wretch" is "allied to you by your own mother, or mother Eve." Echoing Fuller, Fern portrays philanthropy as the bedrock for a newly constructed family—those who need sympathy are her imagined family, if only because they are members of humanity, linked by the common ancestry of Eve. To make her point, Fern satirically mimics readers who disown this family by huffing sanctimoniously, "People shouldn't *get* poor; if they do, *you* don't want to be bothered with it."[11] Fern's condemnation of this smug attitude resonates through her sarcastic tone, and, as does Fuller in some of her work, she implicates readers in contributing to the conditions of poverty. If the title of the article would initially imply that philanthropy itself is "mistaken," Fern's satirical tone makes clear that readers who reject fellow feeling are themselves woefully "mistaken" because of their unsympathetic natures, which are, in part, responsible for worsening the conditions of poverty.

A similar plea for sympathy is evident in "The Charity Orphans." Fern's narrator, accompanied by a friend, observes a line of "charity children" who pass "with closely cropped heads, little close-fitting sun-bonnets and dark dresses." Fern constructs a nested narrative framework as the reader observes the newspaper writer/narrator and her friend as they, in turn, gaze upon the children, who inspire genuine sympathy in one observer and only superficial sympathy in the other. After the friend casually remarks that the orphans constitute a "pleasant sight," the narrator counters, "It takes something more than food, shelter and clothing, to make a child happy," for "its little heart, like a delicate vine, *will* throw out its tendrils for something to *lean on*—something to *cling* to," namely the observer's, and by extension the reader's, sympathy.[12] While her friend views the line of institutionalized children in a detached way, Fern's narrator pushes both her and the audience to examine the orphans more closely, to look beyond the quaintly aesthetic quality of their appearance and embrace the "little heart" that needs far more than food or clothing.

In her confrontation of the friend in "The Charity Orphans," Fern reveals a favorite theme: that unsympathetic or superficially sympathetic readers shoulder a share of responsibility for social problems. The title of the 1864 *New York Ledger* article "Whose Fault Is It?" opens the question of personal and social responsibility and champions self-inspection as readers vicariously stroll through a depressing slum:

> It was a warm day; there were slaughter-houses, with pools of blood in front, round which gambolled pigs and children; there were piles of garbage in the middle of the street, composed of cabbage stumps, onion-skins, potato-parings, old hats, and meat-bones, cemented with cinders, and penetrated by the sun's rays, emitting the most beastly odors. Uncombed, unwashed girls, and ragged, fighting lads swarmed on every door step, and emerged from narrow, slimy alleys. Weary, worn-looking mothers administered hasty but well-aimed slaps at draggled, neglected children, while fathers smoked, and drank, and swore, and lazed generally.
>
> It was a little piece of hell.

Fern draws a rich, almost novelistic picture, a scene that figuratively (and, she hopes, literally) immerses her readers in the realities of poverty—its shocking sights, its rank odors, its desperate cacophony. Unlike the Baudelarian flaneur (or, in this case, flaneuse), who prowls city streets for titillating purposes, Fern prods her audience to *feel* social problems even as she, the independent observer, sees, smells, hears, and feels the pain of "uncombed, unwashed girls," "ragged, fighting lads," and "weary, worn-looking mothers." Her deeply descriptive voice animates the slums, but she strives for more than the superficial pity one might feel when reading about this type of street in a novel before closing the book's cover and continuing with a self-absorbed daily life. Fern requires readers to reflect on their own inaction in addressing the conditions she lays before them. The wealthy—those responsible for "corporation-dinners, . . . Fourth of July fireworks, and . . . public balls, where rivers of champagne are worse than wasted"—are partially responsible for conditions that will "slay more victims than the war is doing" and kill more people than the disease and despair of the slums themselves. "There must," she concludes, "be horrible blame somewhere for such a state of things on this beautiful island," and she centers that blame on readers who care more for their own social position than for the well-being of their neighbors.[13]

The indifferent wealthy come under attack again in an article about working girls. The "observing stranger who walks" the city streets notes "the contest between squalor and splendor" presented in the pairing of the "care-worn working-girl" and the "dainty fashionist." Taking the reader—perhaps a "dainty fashionist" herself—by the hand, Fern commands that she join the journalist and "follow [the girls] to the large, black-looking building, where several hundred of them are manufacturing hoop-skirts" in a "deafening" factory. "*You*," the eventual wearer of the under garment, "could not stay five minutes in that room," yet Fern insists that the reader stand beside her and "observe" the girls "as you enter."[14] The reporter situates fashion—embellishment of the private self—in public terms. The "fashionists" dress extravagantly, but that clothing ultimately envelops a space far beyond the enclosure of their own bodies. Acts of personal adornment have social consequences, for, in emphasizing the superficial self, individuals turn blindly away from the sordid city factories where their clothing is fashioned. Fern insists that her readers look and feel, so they might observe the sufferings of those factory girls through the mediation of a sympathetic reporter. Foregrounding a topic women are supposed to enjoy—in this case, fashion—Fern turns the picture of the "feminine" self into a treatise on the relationship between the private woman and the working (public) girls. In the process, her piece mocks and subverts articles about fashion and the colored plates that show the latest styles within many women's magazines; suddenly, the latest styles have become emotionally and socially suspect. The display of wealth cloaks and smothers sympathy.

INSTITUTIONAL HOMES

Nowhere do we see Fern's insistence on sympathetic identification more vividly than in her articles on imprisonment and madness. In the 1856 "Peeps from under a Parasol," a piece Fern revised for her 1857 book *Fresh Leaves,* readers stroll alongside Fern's narrator as she traverses the city and "peeps" at the carnival of activity unfolding on the streets. One scene in particular attracts her attention: that of a "young girl . . . struggling in the grasp of two sturdy policemen." The incident draws a crowd of men and boys, who heckle the unfortunate woman: "Boys shouted; men, whose souls were leprous with sin, jeered," while the women in the crowd, "heartless and scornful," "passed by on the other side" of the street. The alleged criminal serves as a spectacle of amusement and the target of scorn as the crowd, as well as the reader, gazes on her agony, made visible to all. But while the onlookers see the conflict as a source of entertainment, Fern turns her reader's attention inward, toward the heart of sympathy. Unlike the "heartless" women in the sketch, she models a feminized ethos of emotion, suggesting that she, simultaneously the "reader" of the scene and its journalistic creator, can provide critical insight into what she sees from "under the parasol." This accused woman, guilty of a crime or not, is "goaded to madness by the gathering crowd," and she "seize[s] her long trailing tresses, and tossing them up like a veil over her shame-flushed and beautiful face, resign[s] herself to her fate."[15]

Fern rhetorically unveils and then re-veils the woman. She, the newspaper woman observing the incident, is not particularly concerned about whether or not this woman is a criminal. What does concern her, however, is how the woman stands before the public, "shame-flushed" and exposed, as if she is a suspect drawn directly from the pages of the *Police Gazette,* animated for the enjoyment of the goading crowd. The newspaper woman can detect—and thus convey in print—something no one else bothers to observe: the sad figure's humanity. Drawing herself and her readers into the dramatic moment, Fern muses that perhaps an "unfriended" life has driven this wretch to crime. She becomes the sympathetic mediator of the scene, arguing for a sympathetic identification that permits not only the female reporter but, through her, the audience to do far more than peep at the woman with base derision.[16] She asks them, in a sense, to peer beyond what the woman *appears* to be.

Fern follows this pattern of sympathetic identification in two of her articles about Blackwell's Island, and, like her predecessor Fuller, she reserves some of her angriest words for descriptions of public institutions. Her calls for reform hinge once again on the act of self-reflection, as depicted through her own gendered journalistic observations. As Fern travels through the Blackwell's Island prison, she places herself in the role of observer, an initially unaffected visitor who, in keeping with the formula of other articles, notes the island's beautiful setting. However, diverging sharply from the entertaining nature of many other prison-visit stories, Fern's initial reaction to the island's natural beauty—the public face of the prison—turns to shock as she enters the building and senses the prisoners' "shining eyeballs peer[ing] at my retreating figuring through the grating." Reversing the gaze of the visitor—and of the newspaper reader—Fern grants agency to the prisoners. They now become spectators watching the public as it invades their "home," seeking impersonal entertainment. The redirection of the observational lens makes Fern reflective. "I say this is *not* the way to make bad men good," she emphasizes—sympathy will go farther than objectification and debasing punishment.[17]

Fern realizes, however, that readers may reject her message as uninformed, unreasonable, mawkish, *womanly*. She dispatches that argument forcefully: "You may tell me that I am a woman, and know nothing about it; and I tell you that I *want* to know. I tell you, that I don't believe the way to restore a man's lost self-respect is to degrade him before his fellow-creatures; to brand him, and chain him, and poke him up to show his points, like a hyena in a menagerie." In criticizing the methods of punishment and the public display of misery on Blackwell's Island, Fern attacks readers who might draw voyeuristic pleasure from reading about prisons. Her audience might be tempted to view the prisoners, on exhibit within her own articles, as hyenas in a menagerie. But the newspaper woman undercuts that potential objectification with her angry voice: institutional change is necessary, and the path to reform lay through emotional identification. "My heart shrieks out in its pain," Fern anguishes, and therein lies her right to speak as a woman within the pages of the newspaper.[18] Because she understands the prison in sympathetic—and, specifically, feminine—terms, she does indeed "know [something] about it." Her simple "*want*" of knowledge, regardless of gender, marks her as an expert in this question of public policy.

Fern directs her harshest words in this Blackwell's Island article toward an implied, unsympathetic reader, whom she genders specifically. "Do you shrug your shoulders, Sir Cynic," she asks, "and number over the crimes they have committed? Are *your* crimes against society less, that they are written down only in God's book of remembrance?"[19] While Fern criticizes unfeeling women in several articles, here she turns on men who reject her analysis because of her gender and her presumed ignorance of public issues.

Men and women alike come under even sharper attack in another Blackwell's Island article. Here, Fern shifts from observing incarcerated men to studying imprisoned women—in this case, prostitutes—and blames wealthy libertines and the women who protect them for the unfortunates' condition. As a result, a common visit to the women's wards at Blackwell's Island turns into a brisk defense of women's place in the public sphere. Fern first scolds the women who would "take by the hand the polished roué, and welcome him with a sweet smile into the parlor where sit your young, trusting daughters; you, who 'have no business with his private life, so long as his manners are gentlemanly'; you, who, while saying this, turn away with bitter, unwomanly words from his penitent, writhing victim. I ask no leave of you to speak of the wretched girls picked out of the gutters of New York streets, to inhabit those cells at Blackwell's Island." Predators lie everywhere, even in the sanctity of the home, and hence the question of why "fallen women" languish in prison forces a public problem into the private sphere—it demolishes the ideological boundaries between private and public. Mothers must look into the private lives of the potential scoundrels who sit in their parlors, courting their daughters. These mothers defer to the principle of masculine privacy, but their refusal to lift whatever veils cover a man's private life simply leads to another woman's downfall. Fern expresses disgust that the privileged women insist their "sons and daughters" must be kept "ignorant of" the fallen woman's "existence." She has no patience for such rubbish and rudely pushes aside the mothers to get to the business at hand: "Get out of my way while I say what I was going to, without fear or favor of yours."[20]

Unlike these unsympathetic—these *unwomanly*—mothers, Fern confesses that upon viewing the "fallen women" of Blackwell's Island her "heartstrings" feel "tugg[ed]." She lifts the blanket of shame covering the line of girls who "file in" to the prison cafeteria, "two by two, to their meals, followed by a man carrying a cowhide in his hand, by way of reminder." The prison warden serves as a metaphorical substitute for the men who have imprisoned these girls through seduction, and Fern turns her full ire on the double standard that allows them to enjoy "perfect absolution" for preying on vulnerable women. The opportunity to do justice lies in the heart, as she demonstrates: "You *have* something to do with it," Fern insists, calling on her readers to identify with the women and voice their outrage publicly.[21]

As in her first Blackwell's Island article, Fern anticipates complaints about her supposed lack of credential to speak in the pages of the newspaper. She envisions the retorts of her critics, who will charge, "Oh, you don't know anything about it; men are differently constituted from women; woman's sphere is home." Fern bristles at the notion, imploring her readers to explain why a woman's identity is tied to domesticity alone. "I have no faith in putting women in a pound," she declares, "that men may trample down the clover in a forty-acre lot. But enough for that transparent excuse."[22] Fern moves effortlessly from discussing the specific issue of "fallen women," to broader points about gender, justice, and women's place in the public sphere. The problem of the prison involves, surely, a lack of sympathy toward the real victims of prostitution, who have in essence been unjustly incarcerated. Amid the dismissal of uncaring women and the men who commit "libels against womanhood," Fern asserts her own strong identity as a professional journalist with the power of exposé, of making private crimes public. One should note that since it published such a wide range of opinion pieces, the *Ledger* did not always offer such a sympathetic view. An anonymous 1856 article, for instance, decries "the sickly sympathy for criminals which has been so rampant for several years past" and declares that "all this prison-discipline-sympathy business is a premium upon crime."[23] Fanny Fern would likely have had a thing or two to say about that.

Fern's 1854 "This Side and That" likewise contrasts the private luxury of middle-class life with the public suffering of imprisoned women. Casting aside the "hollow show and glitter" of common life and "weary of fashion's stereotyped lay-figures," the reporter embarks on a walk through the city with readers, in search of "Dame Fortune['s] ... other side." Dame Fortune leads her to the infamous Tombs prison, and what she sees there resembles nothing short of a ghastly human zoo: "See them, with their pale faces pressed up against the grated windows, or pacing up and down their stone floors, like chained beasts." Fern, though, will not allow these "chained" humans to amuse her virtual prison visitors. Projecting a sympathetic gaze, she declares, "It is the gifted, and generous, and warm-hearted" visitor—and, by extension, newspaper reader—who hears the "summons" of humankind. One prisoner has attempted to make her cell "look *home-like*," even adding "a crucifix in the corner" in a sincere gesture of piety.[24] In her description, Fern conjures a private haven—the "home-like" individual cell, an ironic *parlor*—onto a stark public space—this is a "home" whose fourth wall is made of open prison bars. The "domestic" is public, open not only to the prison visitor but to the reader who travels the corridors of the Tombs with Fern. In her reportage, the woman's private act of prayer in the corner of an open prison cell becomes a public prayer for sympathy, registered by the female pen.

Fern's survey of prisons continued into the 1870s, when she visited institutions in Plymouth and Richmond. In the Pilgrims' own Plymouth, a place that "does not insure saintliness in all its descendants," she encounters a "woman who had poisoned her husband, when sick and helpless on her hands," as well as mothers imprisoned for "violation of the liquor laws," there with their young children, whose "little waxen face[s] showed signs of severe suffering." Fern's maternal outrage awakens as she confronts this perverse domestic scene, especially when she realizes the women on display must feel intense "bitterness" at the "difference that bright day in our respective lots," despite Fern's heartfelt longing to free, at least, the children. A similar longing results from Fern's visit to Libby Prison in Richmond, when she attempts to look "through its grated, cob-webbed windows, not with *my* eyes, but with the hopeless eyes of hundreds whose last earthly glimpse of the sunlight was through them."[25]

In these articles, her last on prison conditions, Fern extends authorial emotion into a deep act of sympathetic identification. Recognizing the animosity that the incarcerated women in Plymouth must feel when the public plods through their prison "home," she yearns to trade her emotion for theirs, merging her understanding of the mothers' and children's needs with the pain she witnesses, their sufferings behind the grate that literally and verbally separates them. Fern attempts to relinquish her identity so that she can join the prisoners and allow their eyes to become hers; she envisions a radical dismissal of the private self, in fellow feeling with the prisoners on public display.

Fern combines pictures of feminized sympathy and public complaint in most of her articles; the formulation is not unique to her prison writings.

Her 1858 visit to Blackwell's Island included, naturally, a stop at the "lunatic department," which yields yet another example of her sympathy-infused representations of institutional life. At that time, the asylum was under the gentle guidance of a superintendent influenced by a program of moral treatment. Fern praises the "neatly appointed rooms," which commanded" a restorative "view of sea, sky, and woodland, as diverse as beautiful," and a stark "contrast" to the "stupid . . . tyranny" of former eras, "which placed such unfortunate sufferers on par with criminals." Sharp-tongued as ever, Fern curtails the distance between the people on the inside and outside of Blackwell's Island when she observes, "It is curious how each lunatic inevitably hangs to his deluded breast the idea that he is the only sane person in the establishment. (I have known many people out of a lunatic asylum give the same convincing proof of their qualifications to be in it!)."[26]

Each patient Fern meets leads her to ponder humanity's common nature. The asylum patients do not differ fundamentally from anyone else: they simply voice the deep emotions and enact the impulses that people "outside" have learned to suppress out of social convention. One woman, for example, bluntly tells Fern that the newspaper woman can visit for a time, provided she "don't stay too long, and talk too much," a comment that makes the writer wonder what would happen if, in the outside "diplomatic world," a woman "[spoke] out in meetin'" if the minister grew tiresome and long-winded. "I am not at all sure that the wheels of society need be greased with so much fibbing and flattery to keep them from creaking," an amused Fern imagines. Her observation of another patient returns her to the theme of "public domesticity." As she walks along the hospital corridors, she glances through a door into the room of a young woman, who "start[s] to her indignant feet with a tragic 'How dare you?'" Fern undercuts readers' temptation to examine the madwoman as a violent threat, insisting instead that they be aware of the violation *looking* can embody. As Fern reflects, "I was forced to believe that the proverb, 'Every man's house should be his castle,' held as true of the lunatic as of anybody else."[27] It is this recognition of shared humanity as the bedrock for genuine sympathy that typifies all of Fern's writing about prisons and asylums. In rhetorically opening institutional doors, she reiterates the power of—and need for—sympathy, as modeled by the journalist. It is, moreover, a theme she echoes in her first novel, *Ruth Hall,* a meta-fiction about the power of the sympathetic voice of the newspaper woman.

PUBLIC SYMPATHY IN *RUTH HALL*

Of all Fanny Fern's work, the novel *Ruth Hall* has amassed the greatest scholarly attention, and understandably so. A delightfully sly roman à clef, the book traces the title character's personal and professional development from timid wife and mother to self-possessed newspaper woman and public figure. In the novel's opening, Ruth, daughter and sister of cold, foppish men (modeled after Fern's own father and brother), leaves home to marry the loving Harry Hall. Children and domestic security follow, despite the interference of overbearing in-laws. Tragedy strikes, however, when first one child and then Harry dies, leaving Ruth penniless and friendless. Repeatedly rejected by family members who refuse to aid her, Ruth embarks on a frantic search for employment as her living conditions sink to desperate levels. Finally, she finds work in the public sphere of the periodical marketplace, learning along the way to develop and then protect her professional voice. Writing under the nom de plume "Floy," Ruth's success is phenomenal, and she soon earns impressive journalistic capital. Indeed, the novel ends with her signing an exclusive newspaper contract and gaining financial security, symbolized by an engraving of a bank note reproduced in the book's final pages.

Ruth Hall mirrors Fern's own personal hardships and subsequent rise to fame, as I describe in the biographical sketch at the beginning of this chapter (minus, notably, the divorce—Fanny Fern, after all, had a reputation to uphold). Her representations of readily identifiable characters, however, invited outrage among embarrassed family members and unleashed a torrent of criticism against her apparent bitterness over how they had treated her during her troubles. A reviewer in the *New-York Tribune* chided Fern for her breach of polite conduct, while a *London Albion* critic argued *Ruth Hall* was not "creditable to the female head and heart." Other writers implored her to pursue "a more womanly and modest course in her future works." Recognizing the quasi-autobiographical nature of the novel, critics were particularly appalled that Fern sought public vengeance on family members. The *New Orleans Crescent* declared, "As we wish no sister of ours, nor no female relative to show toward us, the ferocity she has displayed toward her nearest relatives, we take occasion to censure this book that might initiate such a possibility."[28] These critical complaints suggest fear of the feminine voice and outrage that a woman might use the platforms of fiction and journalism to write in "unfeminine" ways. This "unfeminine" writing, however, is precisely the quality that drew—and continues to draw—readers to Fern, including men, as Nathaniel Hawthorne's admiring remarks remind us.

Fern directs her sharp narrative tone against negligent family members, but she strategically positions her title character in readily recognizable terms that would be familiar to mid-century readers. Ruth at first exemplifies the ideologically proper stereotype of antebellum true womanhood, with her religiosity, initial subservience to men, moral purity, and domesticity. Further, the plot of *Ruth Hall* upends the pattern of the antebellum sentimental novel, which is marked by a typical plot trajectory—an innocent young woman, often an orphan, must find her way in the world, helped along by her piety, submissiveness, purity, and homemaking prowess. Despite trials and tribulations, the heroine ultimately finds happiness in marriage, her own home, and the promise of children to come. In Fern's hands, however, the sentimental novel grows into a tribute to the professional feminine pen. While exhibiting, initially, all the hallmarks of a sentimental novel, including scenes of marriage and domestic joy, a child's death, and remarkable plot coincidences, *Ruth Hall* radically reverses key components of novelistic convention. Fern situates Ruth's marriage, for instance, not as her ultimate, crowning accomplishment but as the opening scene of the novel, in which Ruth views her imminent nuptials with trepidation and wonders if her happiness will survive the stresses of married life. The bliss of motherhood follows, but it is marked by the realistic pains of childbirth, which leave Ruth unconscious. The scene nicely captures Fern's wry sense of humor:

> Hark! to that tiny wail! Ruth knows that most blessed of all hours. Ruth is a mother! Joy to thee, Ruth! Another outlet for thy womanly heart; a mirror, in which the smiles and tears shall be reflected back; a fair page, on which thou, God-commissioned, mayst write what thou wilt; a heart that will throb back to thine, love for love.
>
> But Ruth thinks not of all this now, as she lies pale and motionless upon the pillow. . . . She cannot even welcome the little stranger.[29]

In language initially florid and maudlin, then stark and realistic, Fern undercuts the most celebratory picture of motherhood; intense pain and even unconsciousness accompany the bliss of birth.

Fern's subversion of sentimental convention suits her purpose perfectly. Ruth finally forges her identity not through marriage and motherhood alone but by crafting a journalistic presence and becoming a celebrated newspaper woman. At the end of the novel, Ruth clutches a bank stock note rather than a new husband's hand. As Fern warns in the book's preface, her work is "entirely at variance with all set rules for novel-writing."[30] She uses the same array of shifting narrative voices—sentimental, satirical, first person, third person—and her chapters fly between brief scenes depicting social climbing, conflict with in-laws, family strife, and death. The multivocal aspect of the novel is entirely in keeping with its interest in the professional female. *Ruth Hall* details the development of a woman's public voice as she journeys from an essentially silent young woman into a figure of strength and volume, through the auspices of her journalistic work.

Ruth's journey from private woman to public figure links two crucial elements: sympathy and newspaper professionalism. As Ruth's fame grows, she refines her sense of fellow feeling, writing about social abjection and advocating for the reform of attitudes toward criminals and the insane. And as her journalistic alter ego, Floy, gains publicity, she is better able to articulate her ethos of sympathy. She models fellow feeling in her writing and consistently forces her readers beyond the private act of reading, toward the recognition of commonality and public responsibility. While Fern omits from the novel reproductions of Floy's columns, she does describe the fan mail Ruth receives, and the audience reaction recorded there suggests how her articles awaken sympathies. One letter exemplifies the reformatory power of her words: "Dear Floy: I am a better son, a better brother, a better husband, and a better father, than I was before I commenced reading your articles."[31] Ruth's newspaper-writing, built on sympathetic identification, holds the power to change the individual, a process that, by implication, will continue to extend outward, into public reform.

Although Ruth's sympathetic gaze features prominently throughout the novel, one particularly memorable episode stands as an example of her sense of fellow feeling: her visit to a mental asylum, where she unexpectedly finds her friend Mary Leon. The scene serves as a fitting example not only for this study, given its focus on madness and crime, but for how Ruth develops her sense of sympathy and learns to vocalize that emotion through journalism. Mary and Ruth had met early in the novel, and at that time Mary revealed her husband's abusiveness. Though seemingly an enviable spouse, Mr. Leon is in fact "a tall, prim, proper-looking person,

... extremely punctilious in all points of etiquette, very particular in his stated inquiries as to his wife's and his horse's health, very fastidious in regard to the brand of his wine, and the quality of his venison." In short, one of the fashionable types whom Fern disdains, he ranks his wife among his possessions, akin to his horse, "fastidiously" cared for but objectified all the same. Ruth feels inexplicably drawn to Mary, and once their relationship blossoms, she learns the truth about her friend's husband. Mary enjoys jewels and a fine wardrobe—"all those pretty toys"—but she lacks her husband's sympathy.[32] Once more, Fern constructs a false domesticity, a horror in the private space of the home.

Mary Leon and Ruth lose contact after Ruth's husband dies, but some time later, Ruth strolls by an "Insane Hospital," whose gatekeeper invites her to enjoy some impromptu tourism: "Want to walk round ma'am? ... [C]an, if you like." Evoking the template for other asylum visit stories published in newspapers and magazines, Ruth first surveys the pleasant exterior of the building, with its "terraced banks, smoothly-rolled gravel walks, plats of flowers, and grape-trellised arbors." Inside, however, Ruth discovers women who have been rejected by their husbands and driven to insanity—one woman's husband "ran away from her and carried off her child with him, to spite her, and now she fancies every footstep she hears is his." The law, it would seem, is "generally ... on the man's side."[33]

Ruth learns that the reprehensible Mr. Leon has, likewise, wrongfully imprisoned his wife in the asylum, claiming it is "for her health" and then departing for a long European tour. Abandoned, Mary has chosen death over captivity. The asylum's unemotional matron, a woman "gaunt, sallow and bony," whose unsympathetic eyes "very much [resemble] those of a cat in the dark," leads Ruth to Mary's corpse, now an "emaciated form" with "sunken eyes and hollow cheeks." She has chosen to die alone rather than be gazed upon by the "careless, hireling eyes" of the asylum staff and curious sightseers.[34] Only Ruth, a woman with genuine sympathy, maintains the capacity to mourn Mary's death, and through her grief, Fern reinforces the centrality of Ruth's sympathy. Coming, as the scene does, just before Ruth embarks on her newspaper career, Fern suggests that the professional writer has the gendered ability to express sympathy toward institutionalized women, some of whom might be, unlike Ruth's friend, saved.

A similar example of sympathy in the face of "incarcerated women" occurs when Ruth and her daughters move to a boardinghouse. From her own squalid room, Ruth surveys the tenement houses across the dingy street, peering into their private spaces through their opened blinds. She sees "at one window" a poor tailor toiling in exhaustion, "at another, a pale-faced woman . . . bent over a steaming wash-tub, while a little girl of ten, staggering under the weight of a basket of damp clothes, was stringing them on lines across the room to dry." Yet another window reveals "a decrepit old woman, feebly trying to soothe in her palsied arms the wailings of a poor sick child." Fern overturns a potentially intrusive moment as Ruth peers into the windows; she watches her neighbors not to pass judgment on them or to take prurient entertainment from what she observes, but to *feel*, just as, presumably, some of her neighbors might look into her own room and identify with her. "Home in the city," as Betsy Klimasmith phrases it, is only semiprivate, especially once poverty and other social problems break down the walls between domesticity and publicity. Fern has already alerted the reader that this kind of intrusion would take place within the covers of her novel. As she warns in her preface, "I have entered unceremoniously and unannounced, into people's houses, without stopping to ring the bell."[35] As always, though, her mission is to "enter unceremoniously" in order to model and nurture sympathetic expression.

While Ruth ponders the street outside her window, her eye lingers on one building in particular, a "pretentious-looking house, the blinds of which were almost always closed." This establishment attempts to keep its domestic quarters private, shielded from the eyes of other city dwellers. However, the house represents only a parody of domesticity, for it admits a stream of men: "Throngs of visitors went there—carriages rolled up to the door, and rolled away, gray-haired men, business men, substantial-looking family men, and foppish-looking young men." Realizing that the neighboring house is a brothel, Ruth agonizes over the women she glimpses inside, some "young and fair," others "wan and haggard," and experiences a rush of emotion for the prostitutes, moral "criminals" whose despair is palpable as they peer outward from the false sanctity of this ironic home.[36] The brothel shelters the prostitutes, but it is a space invaded by a constant flow of strange men rather than doting husbands and brothers—it is a prison rather than a home.

Through Fern's narration, Ruth's eyes serve vicariously as her readers', and she serves as the mediator who prompts their sympathies. In short, Fern places Ruth's sympathy on display, a pattern that continues throughout the novel as she begins to understand that the private pain she feels when she observes the "public women" must find, in turn, a public outlet. As in the many articles that feature Fern inviting readers to accompany her in walks around the city, the novel's city scene becomes one more stop on Ruth's journey to find her own sympathetic voice.

The porous boundaries between public and private, as enacted in this chapter of the novel, reflect the sympathetic reaction and action Fern desires of her readers as they move from individual reflection to more substantive expressions of sentiment. Floy travels from the domestic space to the literary platform through the medium of the newspaper, breaking the "rules" of women's writing as she does so, along with the "rules" about what kind of writing women can do in the first place. One newspaper office Ruth visits in her early attempts to find work, for instance, may as well sport a "no women allowed" sign over its door. As she timidly enters the office, she notes "a group of smokers, who, in slippered feet, and with heels higher than their heads, were whiffing and laughing, amid the pauses of conversation, most uproariously."[37] The male journalists eventually acknowledge her with "a rude stare" and dismiss her promptly; women need not apply. The newsroom excludes Ruth, yet she insists on her right to speak through this masculine medium, and in turn Fern presents multiple interactions between public and private through the mediating eye of reportorial sympathy.

Fanny Fern's strident defense of a public, professional voice ultimately came at some cost within an American society increasingly invested in the phenomenon of journalistic celebrity—a celebrity magnified in the character of Nellie Bly. As Warren recounts, "celebrity hunters followed [Fern] on the streets, pointing her out and rudely staring at her . . . ; men pretended familiarity with her; souvenir hunters tried to get into her house; and autograph hunters harassed her with constant requests for autographs."[38] Others continued to cast "slurs on her reputation," leaving her "with few women willing to risk friendship."[39] Whether she wished for it or not, Fern's life provoked the kind of spectacle about which she complained in her articles and novels.

Still, Fern's fame proves instructive when read in the context of her journalism and her journalistic novel. These works exemplify how she used her writing to "influence public policy, not simply private behavior," including how outsiders interacted with lunatics and criminals.[40] As such, she transgressed ideological strictures that limited her sympathetic expression to the home and instead accented it in the pages of the newspaper, serving as a mediator as her audience joined her in properly "reading" public institutions and the people kept inside them. In the process, she crafted her own professional space within a newspaper marketplace that still, like the dismissive newspaper men in *Ruth Hall,* might cast a "rude stare."

Fern's career stretched into the 1870s, and her writing about incarcerated and institutionalized women serves as a bridge to the final portions of this study, the last two decades of the nineteenth century, when women gained ever-greater opportunities to pursue careers in newspaper journalism, thanks in large part to figures like Fern. However, these newspaper roles problematized the construction of journalistic sympathy, especially as it pertained to interactions with madness and crime.

CHAPTER 4

Making a Spectacle of Herself

Nellie Bly, Stunt Reporting, and Marketed Sympathy

I had but little sympathy for these women who do wrong.

—Nellie Bly, "In the Magdalen's Home,"
New York World, February 12, 1888

In October 1893, Nellie Bly published a column that, like most of what she wrote, drew an appreciative audience among readers of Joseph Pulitzer's *New York World*. She had interviewed an accused murderer, a woman named Lizzie, from Monticello, New York, but unlike another Lizzie who enjoyed much greater fame in 1893—the infamous Lizzie Borden, who had been acquitted of the murders of her father and stepmother just four months earlier—this one, Eliza Brown Halliday, had been arrested in September for the murders of her husband, Paul (some forty years her senior), a domestic helper named Margaret McQuillan, and McQuillan's daughter Sarah. Numerous articles in the New York dailies supplied all the sordid and appalling details readers demanded, lingering over such gruesome scenes as the discovery of the McQuillan bodies decomposing under a pile of hay in Lizzie's barn, and, even more shockingly, Paul Halliday's corpse rotting under the kitchen floor in a grotesque echo of Poe's "Tell Tale Heart."

When Lizzie Halliday moved into the idyllic New York village, she brought with her a decidedly checkered past, and soon an array of provocative stories—some rumor, some true—circulated among townspeople: she had started fires in the family home; she had once been committed to an insane asylum; she was a gypsy; she was a thief. By the time police placed her in custody, the citizens of Monticello and the readers of the *World* wanted the answer to a critical question: Was Lizzie Halliday raving mad, or was she only feigning madness? One journalist charged that she "exhibited almost all of the feints and resources usually gone through with ignorant people who are endeavoring to feign insanity."[1] Others weren't convinced and speculated that her appalling violence might, in fact, be symptomatic of a hopelessly disturbed mind. At the time Nellie Bly finally gained entrance to the accused woman's cell in October, no other reporter had been able to draw out the truth, and she sought from Halliday either a full confession or an outright denial of the crime. What she got instead was confrontation with a woman who froze "the blood in one's veins and banish[ed] all feeling of human sympathy," a woman whose "cool, cunning" and "small pig's eyes betrayed the workings of her remarkably shrewd brain."[2]

Despite Bly's less than flattering representation in her *World* article, Halliday offered another interview with the famous reporter just two weeks later. Bly readily accepted, bringing along an artist who vividly illustrated the resulting article, "A Woman without a Heart," by depicting the solidly built Halliday behind bars, hunched over a copy of the *World* that is opened, naturally, to a story about herself (see fig. 6). This time Bly's interviewing efforts proved more fruitful, and they made for some spectacular copy. Halliday admitted to witnessing the murders but maintained that an unidentified gang had carried them out after first assaulting her. She also confessed to six marriages, several of which had ended when her husbands suddenly and mysteriously expired—and some of which also seemed to overlap in time.

In its sheer sensationalism, Halliday's story seemed handcrafted to quench the thirst for drama among the *World*'s readers, as had the story of the other famous Lizzie in 1893. Unlike Borden, however, this Lizzie could not rely on prominent social status to bolster her claims of innocence. Nor, for that matter, did she enjoy a particularly sympathetic interviewer. Placing herself within her own article, Bly posed as the shrewd investigator who would uncover the cunning Lizzie's lies, and she asserted with conviction that the prisoner's "only concern is to get all the things she thinks belong to her. She is, in short, the most avaricious woman I ever met." Bly cast herself in nearly literary terms, a crafty female Sherlock Holmes who turns on the accused and says, "Lizzie Halliday, do you know what I believe? I believe that you alone and unaided killed your husband and the McQuillan woman and buried them. I don't believe you were ever insane one moment

MRS. HALLIDAY IN HER CELL IN THE MONTICELLO VILLAGE JAIL.

Figure 6. Nellie Bly's articles about Lizzie Halliday were accompanied by images of the accused woman, like this one from October 22, 1893, depicting Halliday in her cell, reading none other than the *New York World*. (University of Arkansas Libraries, Fayetteville)

in your life, and that you are the shrewdest and most wonderful woman criminal the world has ever known."[3] In the end, Bly's reaction seemed justified. A jury convicted Halliday of murder and sentenced her to death by electrocution, though a judge later commuted the sentence and sent her to live out her days at New York's Mattawan State Asylum, citing the prisoner's clear mental instability.[4] Lizzie Halliday, it turned out, was raving mad after all.

Bly's articles splashed lurid details onto the front pages of the newspaper, and the newspaper woman trumpeted her own role in the story, spotlighting herself not only as the interviewer who would work tirelessly to "get a scoop" but as a pivotal character in the drama, the heroine who would brave the prisoner's "shrewd brain" and determine innocence or guilt. Bly became the one journalist who could crack the code of the murderer, a feat all the more remarkable because of her supposedly frail gender. If Fern envisioned herself as the bridge between the unfortunate figures in her articles and a public she had tutored in sympathy, Bly configured a new type of sympathy, supported by dramatic shifts in the roles a few fearless women would play for major urban dailies. Her position demanded that she serve less as a moral model for readers as they sought to identify (or not) with the subjects of the reporter's stories. Rather, her work tended to subordinate the words and feelings of an article's ostensible subject (in this case, Lizzie Halliday) and redirect readers' attention toward the reporter herself, the brave and skillful professional woman who would deliver the scoop to a sensation-hungry readership. By reporting on madness and crime, Bly followed in the footsteps of Fuller and Fern, both of whom appear within their articles as active observers of people in prisons and asylums. Bly, however, expanded the newspaper woman's role in her writing and formulated a distinctive style. She was not necessarily a sympathetic observer of pathetic scenes but an active participant, through a narrative framework that emphasized the newspaper woman's presence not as a tool for directing readerly sympathy toward distressed subjects but for celebrating the reporter herself, who often *posed* as a distressed figure. Bly, in other words, took sympathy public and marketed it as a feature of a "new journalism."

From the start of her career with the *New York World,* Bly cultivated an identity based on her performance of daring undercover stories, acting at various times as, for example, a working girl, a thief, and child trafficker. In the thrilling newspaper stories that followed each exploit, Bly consciously made a spectacle of not only the subjects of the story but herself as heroine within these manufactured dramas. Readers turned to her articles for the thrill of watching her overcome obstacles and, frequently, interact with undesirables—in the process, winning her audience's admiration and sympathy. In comparison with the other figures in this study, Bly's sympathy seems at times self-referential: readers identified with, and invariably admired, the newspaper woman, who made news happen and was herself the news. I wish to complicate, in this chapter, the story of Bly's career by diverging from other journalism historians, who often identify in her work a deeply sympathetic and crusading spirit. While Bly unquestionably stands as a pivotal figure in the history of women's journalism, I scrutinize her writing about asylums, madness, prisons, and crime with an eye toward how her

uses of sympathy functioned within an increasingly profit-driven, trivializing, and sensationalistic periodical marketplace. The rhetorical strategies
evident within these articles resonate against the journalism of Fuller, Fern,
and Jordan. In my analysis, Bly's presentation of herself as the central sympathetic figure in her stories, battling against New York's frightening public
institutions, served as a tool by which she could reinforce her professional
status. Bly's redirected sympathy highlights the opportunities available to
female journalists at the end of the century and adds complexity to the story
of sympathy on the pages of the urban newspaper.

This chapter explores two of Bly's stories about spectacle and marketable sympathy, starting with the project that turned her into a household
name: posing as a madwoman and going undercover into the asylum on
Blackwell's Island. I then examine a similar reportorial stunt, in which Bly
arranged her own arrest in order to assess New York's jail system from behind bars. In both cases, a daring new type of newspaper woman emerges as
rightful recipient of her audience's sympathetic gaze. The reporter acts not
as an example to instruct readers how to sympathize with social outcasts,
but a leading actress in her own literary drama—a heroine precisely because
she is *not* insane, *not* a criminal. Reading these articles alongside those of
Fuller, Fern, and Jordan adds texture to Bly's brand of professionalism, one
that would in her time influence how some women could break into the
masculine stronghold of the "city room." It was, ultimately, writing built
on feminine publicity and the reporter who moved outside the confines
of private, domestic spaces in dramatic, unprecedented ways.

New Journalism and Newspaper Women in the Late Nineteenth-Century News Room

A precise picture of women's professionalization in late nineteenth-century
New York newspaper journalism requires readers to delve into the world
of 1880s and 1890s "new journalism"; Nellie Bly and Elizabeth Jordan both
contributed to and were supported by this game-changing development
in modern newspaper journalism. Since the 1830s, a division had grown
between inexpensive dailies that catered to working-class readers—publications like the *New York World*—and more expensive, somber periodicals
like the *New York Evening Post* and the *New York Times*. Joseph Pulitzer,
first at the *St. Louis Post-Dispatch* and then at the *World*, popularized in his

papers a profitable mixture of sensationalism, human interest, and visual interest for the mass, urban market, which had been dominated by relatively staid papers following the Civil War. Even though the *World* and similar newspapers principally featured "hard news," that news stood on a sturdy scaffolding of drama and on a reporting style that sought "to shock readers with graphic detail and satisfy an appetite for the obscene, erotic, or bizarre."[5] This "new journalism," as it was called, privileged stories that tantalized and *sold,* as even a glance at just a few headlines makes evident: "They Died in Sin," "She Was Crazed by Terror," "She Fought Three Wildcats," "An Eight Year Old Wife," "Whose Hand Held the Ax?" "Scenes in an Opium Joint."[6]

An 1897 feature in *Outlook* magazine titled "The Condemned Journalism" encapsulates, satirically, the ethos of new journalism by imagining how a Pulitzer-style paper would report the infamous case of Charles Lamb's mad sister, Mary, who, in a fit of manic frenzy, murdered their mother in 1796. The London reports of the time conveyed basic information about the tragic event in even, nondramatic language and refused to "[gloat] over the scenes" or even to name the suspect, declaring that the family's "grief was too sacred to be paraded before the public as a bit of entertaining news."[7] New journalism, in contrast, would scoff at this sobriety and circumspection, as the article observes in a delightful passage worth quoting at length:

Now consider how the "new journalism" would treat such an affair. The first page would be chiefly occupied by illustrations and flaring headlines. The main picture would show the tragedy itself, the daughter driving the knife to her mother's heart, with the father and son rushing to drag her off. Supplementary to this would be small cuts showing: "The knife with which the deed was done—full size;" "The mother as she looked in life;" "X-ray photograph showing the knife passing between the ribs and reaching the heart;" "The murderess being strapped down by young Lamb and a neighbor;" "The grief-stricken brother;" "The father;" "The house in which the crime was committed." The "story" would contain interviews with each member of the family, written to order by trained perverts, and there would be veiled hints of a shocking scandal or some hidden motive which led to the deed. Within a week, one of the women of the "new journalism" would have gained access to the place where the maniac was confined and secured an interview with her—or would have claimed as much—and one of the male sleuths would have discovered and published that Charles Lamb himself had been confined in a madhouse but a short time before. Names not mentioned! Grief too sacred to be entertaining! There would have been no detail of the family history or the tragedy, however painful, however ghoulish, however revolting to decency, that the "new journalism" would not have paraded.[8]

Though hyperbolic, this amusing description offers an uncannily accurate prediction of how new journalism actually *would* approach the Lamb story. It would see the family as fresh meat to feed the hungry masses; it would find the spiciest language to enthrall readers; it would, in short, turn personal tragedy into magnificent and entertaining news.

Unsurprisingly, conservative critics assailed the florid style that typified this reportage. Critiquing Pulitzer's work, Matthew Arnold coined the phrase "new journalism" in 1887, remarking that it "has much to recommend it. It is full of ability, novelty, variety, sensation, sympathy, generous instincts." However, he added, its "one great fault is that it is *feather-brained*. It throws out assertions at a venture because it wishes them true; does not correct either them or itself, if they are false; and to get at the state of things as they truly are seems to feel no concern whatever."[9] Another writer charged that new journalism "gradually befouls, perverts, and debases the reader's mind until he is without power to tell good from bad."[10] Other critics were even more pointed, as this doggerel from an 1897 issue of *Life* magazine suggests:

Sixty-nine pages of rubbish,
Twenty-two pages of rot,
Forty-six pages of scandal vile,
Served to us piping hot. . . .
Thirty-four sad comic pages,
Printed in reds, greens and blues;
Thousands of items we don't care to read,
But only two columns of news.[11]

Arnold and other commentators wondered where serious news had gone, and as the century drew to a close and the excesses of new journalism ran ever wilder, they directed their outrage toward newspapers like Pulitzer's *World,* with its steady attention to the city's most marketable dramas.

Arnold may have dismissed new journalism as "feather-brained" and unsuitable for the thoughtful reader, but in terms of market viability, the *World* proved once again that sensation sells and that a popular audience translates into solid financial success. As one essayist put it, new journalism would "flourish as long as it pays."[12] And newspaper women became a key strategy in making that journalism pay. By the 1880s, hoary traditions that excluded women from newspaper staffs had begun to soften, and major urban papers might include as many as six women on their full-time rosters, with perhaps twice as many employed casually as correspondents, paid on space rates.[13] The rise of an emergent, female-centered journalism in the 1880s and 1890s reinforced the increasing presence of women in the newsroom.[14] Mainstream publishers recognized that women constituted a virtually untapped reading and purchasing market, and in the never-ending pursuit of advertisers, they aimed more content toward topics they presumed women would enjoy, like Pulitzer's "Fair Woman's World" section. This feature focused on child-rearing, fashion, society news—or, as one subhead put it, "Fads, Fashions, and Foibles of Fair Femininity"—topics deemed proper for "fair women."[15] Additionally, Pulitzer realized that the novelty of female reporters, writing about beats women did not typically cover, like the unseemly elements of city life, could generate enormous publicity and circulation. Rather suddenly, newspaper women became front-page news, through both the articles they wrote and their own participation *in* those articles. Their names appeared within the bold, stacked headlines of the papers, establishing the newspaper woman as a modern type of celebrity.[16]

Despite the development of women's pages and features catering to female readers, women did not gain entrance into the city room without difficulty. Some editors, critics, and readers still considered women fundamentally incapable of reporting hard news. In an early instructional manual for budding journalists, Edwin Shuman warned that as long as formal education trained women principally for the "parlor and the ballroom," they could not function in the manly sphere of the daily city newspaper. While aspiring women wondered if "fashions and society gossip—these husks of frivolity" were "the best that you can offer us on the large city journal?" Shuman concluded that, indeed, those topics were "about all for which the average woman's training has fitted her."[17] Men, in contrast, boasted education in the disciplines of business and politics, "the body and breath of journalism." Clearly, journalism belonged to them, not women. Shuman admitted that a few exceptional women already had secured positions on urban newspapers, but he warned that "much of the work is too arduous, too exhausting, and for the most part too rude in its requirements for the gentler sex," adding that "the amount of nervous strain and concentrated mental and physical energy demanded at the editorial desk are things for which women as a rule are not fitted by nature." Even when women did overcome the "natural" strain and write for the dailies, readers would not expect them to produce much more than "superficial and frothy" articles, the kind of "funny or pathetic or sentimental things that women see where men do not."[18] And these sentimental "things," Shuman concluded, might be sweet, but they were decidedly not "real" journalism.

Pulitzer, Stunt Women, and Nellie Bly

Shuman evidently never met Nellie Bly. She and other newspaper women did not take kindly to the prejudice that they were limited to "superficial and frothy" topics, and new journalism provided a platform on which to prove it. In retrospect, Bly seemed tailor-made for Pulitzer's journalism. Born in 1864, twenty-one-year-old Elizabeth Cochran barged into a journalism career by submitting to the *Pittsburg Dispatch* a sharp-tongued retort to a recently published article titled "What Girls Are Good For."[19] The piece had mocked women's ambitions to enter the public, working world and argued that women could not succeed in any career outside the home. Cochran's pointed response impressed the *Dispatch* editor. Won over by her saucy style and plucky attitude, he offered her a position as reporter. She enthusiastically accepted the job offer and adopted the pen name "Nellie Bly," taken from the popular Stephen Foster song "Nelly Bly." For two years she regaled Pittsburgh audiences with her gutsy style. Breezy and progressive, her pieces carried readers along as she guided them through such adventures as a visit to Pennsylvania's Western Penitentiary and a trip through Mexico, where her articles so annoyed government officials that they asked her to leave. Regardless of her success in Pittsburgh, in the fall of 1887 Bly's ambition led her, nearly penniless and without secure prospects, to New York City, where she "felt ready to crash the gates" of mass media.[20]

Despite the advances of Fuller, Fern, and other journalists, the newspaper world of 1887 was still not a hospitable location for women, whose supposed delicacy made them theoretically incapable of covering topics like crime, politics, economics, and scandal. Their reporting on "soft" women's issues might secure a job on the newspaper staff, but it certainly wouldn't grant easy access to the coveted city room, where the real action and excitement lay. Undaunted, Bly charged into the inner sanctum by publishing in the *Dispatch* an article about women in New York City journalism. Her research for the piece brought her to editors' offices across the city and led to an article that "read like a feminist's lament." Women in the newsrooms, the editors almost universally declared, "are no good, anyway," for their accuracy was questionable, and they were too delicate to handle serious beats.[21] In a beautiful twist of fate, the strength of Bly's story landed her another, more substantive interview with John Cockerill, managing editor of Pulitzer's *World*. Cockerill proposed a startling "test" for the ambitious Bly—she was to arrange to have herself committed, somehow, to the infamous Insane Asylum for Women on Blackwell's Island and to "chronicle faithfully the experiences [she] underwent" there.[22] The assignment was to be a trial by fire for the young reporter, testing her mettle in the cutthroat business of late nineteenth-century urban journalism. Bly met the challenge, and the remarkable story that emerged from the experience proved to be her triumphant introduction to an enormous, rapt audience within New York, and beyond.

In proposing Bly's undercover visit to the asylum, *World* editors were not breaking entirely new ground; earlier reporters had already gone incognito to expose the deplorable conditions within asylums, in an era when the admirable philosophies of moral treatment had fallen to the wayside. Reporter Julius Chambers had been among the most famous; he spent four days in the Bloomingdale Asylum in 1872 and then shared his findings in the pages of the *New-York Tribune*.[23] An English reporter also assumed the role of an "amateur maniac" for three days in 1884, to gain an insider's view of private asylum abuses. Amusingly (and appropriately), an article recounting this exploit references a different case, in which "an old New York newspaper man ... one morning found himself in striped uniform on Blackwell's Island, without any very clear ideas as to how or why he was there." Fortunately, he gains release when a group of asylum tourists includes one of his acquaintances. The reporter's friend mistakenly concludes, however, that he is in the madhouse to do some undercover work and hence praises him for what she assumes is his "professional enterprise and philanthropy in undergoing such discomforts that he might be able to lay before the readers of his newspaper an accurate account of life behind the bars."[24]

Even by 1887, it would seem, Bly's stunt verged on cliché. And by 1897, following Bly's own sensational pieces, cliché degenerated into satirical absurdity in "An Escaped Lunatic," published in the humor magazine *Life*. In this piece "one of the patients from the asylum of New Journalism on Newspaper Row" escapes the madhouse of the city room and, "with the cunning peculiar to the insane," seeks "admission to the Bellevue Pavilion" on Blackwell's Island. The reporter is almost successful in defecting to the city hospital—by implication far superior to the hopeless wards within the newspaper buildings, and the Blackwell's commissioner expresses "much [horror] at the informal methods of admittance to the pavilion, which exposed it" to the danger of deranged escapee journalists. Clearly, the commissioner concludes, "this was the first move in a carefully devised scheme to transfer the entire institution on Newspaper Row to the asylum at Blackwell's, and thus saddle the whole enormous expense of its maintenance upon the City government."[25]

Precedent aside, in asking a woman to perform this undercover work, editors at the *World* inaugurated a type of reporting—and a type of reporter—that became, for a time, nearly synonymous with female newspaper journalists—the "stunt girl." Indeed, the journalistic "stunt," especially when performed by newspaper women, was eventually one of the defining features of new journalism. The reporter would insinuate herself, often anonymously, into a sensational or scandalous situation—a dodgy business enterprise, a daring new fad, an off-limits sporting event, a criminal locale, a racing trip around the world—and bring out of the experience a dramatic, entertaining story that would usually grace the pages of the Sunday *World*. As Bly's biographer remarks, "it was the advent of the stunt girl," epitomized by Bly, alongside "the large separate women's sections" in newspapers "that created the first real place for women as regular members of the newspaper staff," bringing "women, as a class, out of the journalistic sideshow and into the main arena." For women who longed to escape the confines of the women's pages the "new, wild-side genre of 'stunt' or 'detective'" reportage offered a fast ticket, at least for a lucky few, to the front pages and to possible celebrity status along the way.[26]

Stunt reporting coincided nicely with Pulitzer's conception of what William Randolph Hearst would later call "the journalism that acts." By the time Bly joined the *World* staff, the paper sported headlines that trumpeted its skill in *making* the news: solving cases the city police had given up on, acting as rescuers for people affected by natural disasters . . . no objective observer, the journalist participated in—or even manufactured—the news. Bly's stunts "frequently followed the same pattern" of news making. She "would apply for a job or get herself imprisoned and write about her experiences," much to the delight of the loyal newspaper audience.²⁷ A glance at headlines from Bly stories in the late 1880s signals her accomplishments: "Trying to Be a Servant," "Shadowed by a Detective: Nellie Bly Makes a Test of the Private Spy Nuisance," "A Female Usurer's Trick," "Nellie Bly on a Bicycle," "Nellie Bly Learns to Swim," and, of course, "Behind Asylum Bars" and "Inside the Madhouse."²⁸

PRACTICING MADNESS

Heralded as one of the first and arguably most influential female newspaper stunts, the story of Bly's descent into what had become a hellish madhouse developed into a journalistic feat that surpassed even her editors' heady expectations. Her firsthand tale of asylum life appeared first as two lengthy articles in the Sunday *World,* on October 9 and October 16, 1887, published after she finished her self-imposed tenure in the asylum and revealed to the world what she had been up to. The first of these, "Behind Asylum Walls," describes how Bly hatched her plan to enter the asylum, as an undercover patient, and how her dramatic skill posing as a madwoman led to her commitment in Blackwell's Island. The second article, published the following Sunday under the blazing headline "Inside the Madhouse," describes Bly's ten-day stay on Blackwell's Island, the assortment of odd characters she encountered there, and the perils she faced as a sane woman among lunatics.

Two months later, dime-novel publisher N. L. Munro printed a twenty-five-cent book titled *Ten Days in a Madhouse,* which included two additional Bly features, "Trying to Be a Servant: My Strange Experience at Two Employment Agencies" and "Nellie Bly as a White Slave." Bolstered by the strident calls for reform that Bly added to the book, scholars have characterized her work as muckraking: sensationalistic yet socially driven writing inspired by sincere sympathy toward the women who suffered abuses in the asylum. Comparison of *Ten Days in a Madhouse* with the original

World articles, however, reveals a more complicated picture of sympathy and social engagement. A number of the differences between the newspaper text and the book are relatively minor, such as breaking the original two articles into chapters, adding individual sentences, and rearranging paragraphs. Yet Bly added a few substantial passages as well, in addition to a final chapter that shoehorns the articles into a moralistic call for asylum reform. The book version, in other words, offers something closer to a sympathy-laden story than do the newspaper articles, which fundamentally direct readers' interests and sympathies toward Bly as she bravely navigates the realm of the maniacs. With an eye toward the book revisions, I concentrate here on Bly's text as it appeared in the *New York World.* Her self-characterization in relation to severely ill women reveals how, as a newspaper woman writing in the context of new journalism, Bly directed much of her sympathy toward not the mad but herself as the heroine of a harrowing journalistic adventure—a portrayal that, in turn, bolstered her professional authority within the muscular environment of the *World.*

Bly's October 9 article begins by describing the meeting between Bly and Cockerill in which they hatch their infamous plan. Somehow, Bly will gain entrance to the asylum undercover, "with a view to using a plain and unvarnished narrative" to describe the hospital from a patient's point of view. From the outset, Bly regards madness in superficial, bodily terms. Touting her "own ability as an actress," she determines (correctly, as it turns out) that she need only "act" and "look" insane, and a clear path toward professional success will unfold before her. In focusing on the "look" of insanity, Bly reveals her ignorance about—and even indifference toward—the reality of madness. She admits that she knows nothing about mental illness, "had never been near insane persons before in my life, and had not the faintest idea of what their actions were like," perceptions likely shared by her readers, outside of the images they had consumed through popular literature and journalism.[29] If Fuller and Fern express their desire to look deeply into the eyes of the mad and make that knowledge part of their own sympathetic growth and consequent professionalization, Bly, in contrast, seeks only enough knowledge to pass as a stereotype of madness and to create an impressive story for her paper (and, not coincidentally, earn praise for her personal investigative skills).

Bly thus determines to "enact the part of a poor, unfortunate crazy girl." She will move into a boardinghouse and play the role of lunatic; the strangers there will, in turn, commit her to an asylum in short order. In preparation for this theatrical feat, Bly "practices insanity" in front of a mirror, a scene captured by one of the illustrations that accompany the *World* articles (see fig. 7). "I remembered all I had read of the doings of crazy people," Bly recounts, "how first of all they have staring eyes, and so I opened mine as wide as possible and stared unblinkingly at my own reflection."[30] Bly is so frightened by the concept of lunacy and by her convincing ability to "look crazy" that the sight of her own "mad" face reflected before her "in the dead of night" nearly unnerves her, and she must turn up the gaslight to "raise my courage." Bly bases her "practice" of insanity on the stories her readers have likely encountered in print; her performance of madness is, in fact, almost a parody of the representations one finds in other periodical sources.

Armed with the superficial markers of insanity, Bly goes "out to my crazy business," assumes the false name "Nellie Brown," moves into the boardinghouse, and proceeds to "practice" her "insanity" in front of the residents. It takes only a day to convince the other women of her madness and, along with it, secure an assumption that she is predisposed to violence, even though she does not demonstrate any sort of real derangement or signs of violence while she is at the boardinghouse. She doesn't need to. The housemates' reaction toward "Nellie Brown, the insane girl" implies how readily Americans associated mental illness—or, more precisely, a boilerplate appearance of mental illness—with danger. Repeating such phrases as "everything is so sad" and "all the women in the house [seem] to be crazy," Bly signals to the boarders her supposed mental instability, which they find threatening. "I am afraid to stay with such a crazy being in the house," one cries, while another grumbles, "She will murder us all before morning." One woman even dreams of Bly "rushing at her with a knife in . . . hand, with the intention of killing her" and declares that she "would not stay with that 'crazy woman' for all the money of the Vanderbilts."[31]

Gaining admittance to Blackwell's Island will be easier than she supposed, Bly realizes happily. Indeed, she secretly smiles at the indignant remarks about how dangerous she might be, regarding the comments as evidence of her prowess as an actress (and thus reporter) and her progress toward fulfilling her "delicate mission." As I detail in chapter 1, readers—including the boardinghouse women, obviously—were well versed in similar tales about homicidal lunatics. To cite just one example, the January 12, 1889, *World* reports on a woman who, in an epileptic fit, had been carried off to

NELLIE PRACTICES INSANITY AT HOME.

Figure 7. Nellie Bly's first article about her experiences in the Blackwell's Island asylum depicted the reporter as she "practiced insanity" in preparation to going undercover (*New York World,* October 9, 1887; University of Arkansas Libraries, Fayetteville)

Bellevue Hospital and placed in a locked room with a "maniac." Imprisoned, for all intents and purposes, until a *World* reporter—of course—obtains her release, the woman declares she would not have lived through the night with such a dangerous companion.[32] For this role, at least, Bly merely needs to perpetuate, rather than dispel, unsympathetic pictures of lunacy.

Just as Bly anticipates, the women at the boardinghouse beg police to cart away their undesirable neighbor. For the undercover journalist, however, the drama and suspense have only begun. Now she must perform her "crazy business" in front of a judge, doctors, and—even more problematically— other reporters, who often loiter in the city's courtrooms, hungrily waiting to scoop up the latest interesting news story. The thought makes Bly tremble, for "if there is anyone who can ferret out a mystery it is a reporter. I felt that

I would rather face a mass of expert doctors, policemen, and detectives than two bright specimens of my craft."[33] Fortunately for Bly, on this day no reporters are in the courtroom, and though she barely speaks, a judge rules her insane and even unwittingly provides a romantic backstory for the unfolding tale: he concludes that "Nellie Brown"—who has started answering to "Nellie Moreno"—must be a Cuban maiden of genteel Spanish lineage, suffering from amnesia precipitating from an unnamed trauma that has left her friendless and abandoned in the unforgiving city.

In short order, Bly convinces a doctor—"an insanity expert"—of her illness, and once she is packed off to Bellevue Hospital to await transfer to Blackwell's Island, the most perilous part of her adventure commences. Locked at last in a ward with madwomen, Bly channels the fear that most Americans expressed toward lunacy. In finding herself face-to-face with madness at Bellevue and, soon after, on Blackwell's Island, her apparent narrative objective involves composing a riveting tale about the dangers a sane woman faces when surrounded by certifiable humans. She writes not to convey sympathy for these marginalized people or to trace the negligible line separating the sane from the insane but to stage a melodrama starring the fearless newspaper woman as the sympathetic but endangered heroine. Readers have waited in suspense to see if Bly would convince experts of her insanity. Now they will discover if Bly, "locked up in a cell with a lot of lunatics," will turn into one herself. As the intrepid reporter hears "the most horrible insane cries" rising from Bellevue hospital, readers vicariously feel her "chill at the prospect of being shut up with a fellow-creature who was really insane."[34]

If earlier female journalists viewed their prison and asylum visits as both moral and professional imperatives built on womanly sympathy, Bly positions hers as a job, a "business"—or, as a subhead to one of the articles pronounces, "A Delicate Mission." And that mission depends on using her face and body to create a picture of madness convincing enough that her acting will bring success. Her writing participates in and therefore reinforces stereotypes of madness, sensationalizing them as part of a journalistic project and thus trivializing their plight. When Fuller visited the Bloomingdale Asylum for the Insane, in contrast, she sought to defy public perceptions of madness and to make her audience reconsider the equation of insanity with danger or contagion. Quite the contrary—Fuller's description of a Valentine's Day dance focuses on people who "are happy, all interested. Even those who are troublesome and subject to violent excitement in every-day scenes, show here that the power of self-control is not lost," provided they are treated with sympathy and care.[35] Similarly, Ruth Hall's visit to the asylum, as depicted by Fern, paints sympathy for the women whose life circumstances have led them there. Bly's performance, on the other hand, exploits the caricatures against which Fuller and Fern battle in their writing. She rightly presumes that other people will see her physical characteristics as indicative of madness and therefore of danger. The sympathy Bly provokes depends on the fact that readers know the newspaper woman is *not*, in fact, insane. Sympathy extends, that is, toward the "normal" writer as she endures the unsettling experience of being locked up with the mad.

To be fair, if Bly fails to sympathize with the insane as fully as the other female reporters in this study do, she does comment on the need for—and lack of—"womanly sympathy" within both the hospital and the boarding-house. Criticizing the boarders who "wanted to have some amusement at my expense," she praises one Mrs. Caine, who "displayed true womanly feeling" by trying to comfort poor "Nellie Brown," suggesting that only a "true woman" will express anything other than fear or derision at the sight of insanity.[36] Within the domestic haven of the boardinghouse and the gathering of women who constitute this "family," we see little evidence of the emotional impulse tied, ideologically, to a woman's genetic make-up. A similar exposure of perverted femininity is on display later when a nurse calls a patient a "hussy" and other attendants spend "much of their time gossiping about the physicians and about the other nurses" instead of caring for the patients, and always "in a manner that was not elevating." Bly's October 16 article even sports a sizable subhead denouncing "Nurses Who Swear."[37] How can the insane receive adequate care, Bly seems to ask, when the nurses offer to patients only coarse language and gossip rather than womanly sympathy? Ostensibly, Bly seeks to become this woman of sympathy, who will make the patients' pain public and understandable through her professional voice.

Yet, Bly's text as it appears in the *World* articles does not bear out this sympathy, and she undermines the potential for fellow feeling by posing in a spectacle of madness, an object for the newspaper voyeur to consume uncritically, without sincere regard for the actual inmates of Blackwell's Is-land. Indeed, Bly fails to depict psychotic and manic patients with anything close to sympathy—perhaps unsurprisingly, these terribly ill and delusional women terrify her, as evidenced by her emotions on her first moments in the hospital: "My heart gave a sharp twinge. Pronounced insane by four expert doctors and shut up behind the unmerciful bolts and bars of a madhouse! Not to be confined alone, but to be a companion, day and night, of senseless, chattering lunatics; to sleep with them, to eat with them, to be considered one of them, was an uncomfortable position." Bly's fear of madwomen seems to find confirmation at every turn. Some of the women in the asylum "were chattering nonsense to invisible persons, others were laughing or crying aimlessly, and one old, gray-haired woman was nudging me, and, with winks and sage noddings of the head and pitiful uplifting of the eyes and hands, was assuring me that I must not mind the poor creatures, as they were all mad."[38] Mental illness is a threat crowding in on Bly and invading her physical space, a vaguely sinister presence that extends the story's suspense but does little to provoke the reader's sympathy for anyone other than Bly. Who would possibly want to understand a room full of these inexplicable creatures?

An even more startling moment occurs when Bly strips naked for her bath, in front of the other patients. She discovers that "one of the craziest women in the ward" intends to scrub her, a creature holding a "large, discolored rag in her hands," "chattering away to herself and chuckling in a manner which seemed to me fiendish." Similarly, when a line of the most hopeless cases passes by, "a thrill of horror crept over me at the sight. Vacant eyes and meaningless faces, and their tongues uttered meaningless nonsense."[39] These women, it appears, are scarcely even human. In equating the insane with fiendishness and nonsense, Bly casts herself once again as an endangered romantic heroine, at the mercy of devilish and incomprehensible agents, and she asks readers to cheer her along as she protects herself from such terrible captors.[40] Bly realizes that most of her readers share her view of madness as a threat, and she capitalizes on that opinion.

Bly differentiates here between "nervous conditions" and the more obvious and unsettling symptoms of mania and psychosis as indicators of mental illness. The public would naturally side with Bly in her differentiation between psychotic and manic patients, meaning the disturbingly insane, and the "nervous" patients, who would not necessarily display obvious illness. Edward Shorter remarks that before Freudian analysis, "physicians, and certainly the public, were willing to go along with the fiction" that "nervous" problems were not mental illness.[41] Thus, one of the women Bly befriends admits "she was suffering from nervous debility." Another claims she had been in a medical hospital due to an unidentified illness, but her nephew, "being unable to pay her expenses," committed her to the asylum.[42] A German woman is on the island simply because she cannot express herself in English and confirm her sanity. Bly asks yet another patient if she is "crazy." Of course, the woman denies it and proposes, "We will have to be quiet until we find some means of escape."[43] Other examples of wrongful imprisonment abound, including a "Hebrew" woman who was sent to the Island by her jealous husband, a patient who was simply physically ill and poor, and a chambermaid seized and committed after losing her temper with coworkers. Any one of these patients might, in fact, have suffered from more debilitating and problematic conditions—for instance, the loss of temper might have been an element of mania or even psychosis, assuming the chambermaid was a reliable historian of her own illness. Regardless, the idea of the innocent being held captive makes for a more exciting storyline.

Because these women seem, physically speaking, sane—because they do not display the psychosis Bly and her reading public would obviously associate with all insanity—she labels them "as sane as I was myself."[44] Bly finds it simpler, ultimately, to sympathize with "nervous"—meaning depressed, anxious, and obsessive or compulsive—women rather than those she considers mad, thereby sidestepping the deeper social and medical problems evident in the asylum, and the lack of general public sensitivity that reinforces those problems. Consequently, Bly directs much of her own sympathy toward women who are, in her view, falsely institutionalized. These women are "safe" because she reads them as sane and therefore unable to harm her, and they are easier for both Bly and her readers to understand. Their stories become the grounding force of Bly's narrative, while the truly disturbed and disturbing—people stricken with mania or psychosis—represent the threat against Bly and the other innocents because, as true lunatics, they might corrupt the minds and bodies of unjustly institutionalized women. Unfortunately, cases of wrongful commitment did occur, with dismaying frequency, and far more examples were offered in fictional form. Bly astutely plays up this familiar plotline in her own story.

Bly's dramatization of the falsely institutionalized, a type of captivity narrative, is far from random. In a newspaper era that saw an intimate daily exchange between the conventions of fiction and journalism, Bly turns to familiar literary themes and figures to construct her reportage. Thus, readers not only see Bly and other characters cast as endangered heroines; they also witness scenes of diabolical derangement among lunatics, playful flirtation between Bly and an attractive doctor, a romantic subplot unfolding between another doctor and his nurse (adding a bit of steaminess to the story), a brief escape plan, a secret baby in the basement, a madwoman in the attic, and of course plenty of suspense: Will Bly be found out? Will other newspaper reporters discover and disclose her true intent? Or will Nellie go mad before she can be rescued from this house of horrors?

To add flair to the unfolding drama, Bly plays along with the New York judge's presumption that she is of genteel Spanish heritage, a point the city's reporters seized upon in their search for a good story. Indeed, one of the more curious aspects of Bly's story involves how it came to the public's attention—not just in the *World,* in the articles Bly wrote after her stunt had concluded, but in rival newspapers, which reported on the sad case of an anonymous, crazed young woman who had been discovered at a city boardinghouse and committed to Blackwell's. Numerous articles about the "insane girl" appeared during the entire ten days of Bly's confinement, and once she settled on Blackwell's Island, officials received repeated requests for interviews with her. In an era when newspapers posted stories about Gotham citizens gone mad on a nearly daily basis, the amount of press coverage this story attracted is remarkable. Bly's case stood out; "Nellie Brown" was, quite obviously, not the "usual" lunatic—therefore, apparently, she was worth spreading a great deal of ink over. Reporters for the *Sun, Herald,* and *Evening Telegram* all asked (to quote the *Sun's* headline of September 25), "Who Is This Insane Girl?" and reporters clamored to interview the enigmatic figure.[45] How did a person of such apparent refinement go mad? Did she only have amnesia, as some newspaper reporters speculated? Had she been spurned by a lover and thus forced into lunacy? Was she yet another tragic example of a "public woman," driven mad by her sexual improprieties?

Doubtless, part of the news appeal in Bly's case involved her apparent social class and the press's mistaken assumption that she was a Spanish-speaking Cuban whose name was actually Nellie Moreno. "Nellie Brown," of course, did not correct them, since the assumptions added to her intriguing story. The *Sun* called her "a modest, comely, well-dressed girl of nineteen," while the *Herald* pointed out that she was "nicely attired, showing in her speech and bearing every evidence of having been well educated and tenderly reared amid refined associations."[46] In allowing the public to believe she was of genteel and possibly even noble Spanish descent, Bly donned an aura of socially acceptable exoticism. The Cuban framing positioned her in a fashion calculated to draw sympathy toward her predicament and to redirect attention from the mass of genuine asylum inmates. Careful framing is evident as well when reporters and court officials raise the possibility that Nellie Brown's (aka Nellie Moreno's) amnesia might be the result of having been cruelly drugged by some urban villain.

In her own articles, Bly describes this secondary reporting as an exciting subplot and in the process reinforces her own authority as female newspaper reporter. She draws upon the conventions of the captivity narrative herself, and her story grows into a pseudo-medievalist, gothic captivity narrative as a boat carries her to the gloomy ruins of the asylum, perched on a rocky island, a dark adventure starring Nellie Bly, incognito.[47] At the same time, she frames her writing with a cat-and-mouse motif. In the madhouse articles, other reporters figure as detectives, more capable than the "expert" doctors, who cannot tease out "the Cuban girl's" identity. Reporters are mystery-solvers, crafting the news as they perform solid investigative work, just as Bly does in her Lizzie Halliday stories.

As the mystery of Nellie Brown/Moreno deepens and becomes front-page news in several papers, more reporters contrive to meet her, which makes her "tremble," lest they blow her cover. These journalists, "all so bright and clever"—and, not coincidentally, male—stoke her fears that "they should see I was sane" and blow her cover. The reporters become "untiring" in "their efforts to get something new" about the "Cuban girl," a problem, since some of these men "knew me by sight."[48] The tension inevitably grows as Bly repeatedly dodges interview requests. Will the reporters convince asylum keepers to grant access to Brown/Moreno? Will they solve the mystery with their phenomenal detective work? And will they, in the process, ruin Bly's own story?

In praising her male colleagues, Bly implicitly reinforces the even greater prowess of the female journalist. If these men craft news stories, Bly *creates* the news, and she is thus several steps ahead of even the best of them. She stands as the superior reporter, the one with a beat far more important than teasing out the identity of a mysterious madwoman. While male reporters cannot even get to the bottom of the girl's identity, Bly, as a woman, performs the immersion journalism that yields a story of deeper import, with an impact far weightier than the men's surface reporting.[49] Bly succeeds in protecting her real identity during her ten days on Blackwell's Island and will only reveal her secret on her own terms, once she publishes her own, true story in the *World*. In that self-revelation, she asserts her credentials and superiority as a female reporter. She succeeds, that is, in fooling not only the judge, doctors, and other patients but male reporters as well and claims the ultimate scoop.

Pulitzer's editors reveled in Bly's success—and that of the *World* itself—gloating that their paper's new star reporter had pulled a fast one on the legal system, the medical establishment, and, even more importantly, rival newspapers. Once Bly left Blackwell's and the truth of who Nellie Brown/Moreno came out, the *World* was naturally eager to highlight the degree to which all other papers had been fooled by the cub reporter's stunt, and it rushed to print an article trumpeting the "Widespread Interest Caused by 'The World's' Publication" the day after the first installment of Bly's own narration appeared. On October 10, for instance, the day after "Behind Asylum Walls" appeared, the *World* featured a piece called "Nellie Brown's Story," which summarized the "widespread interest caused by 'The World's' publication" and recorded the embarrassed reactions of officials at Bellevue Hospital and Blackwell's Island, all of whom had, after all, locked away a perfectly sane woman.[50] Similarly, an October 15, 1887, article crowed, with more than a little pride, "All the Doctors Fooled"; afterward, in preparation for the second Bly feature, scheduled for publication the following day, health professionals scrambled to defend themselves.[51] Bly penned her own response to a *Sun* story that had questioned the validity of her claims, once again marking her professional credentials.[52] And at least one clever merchant seized on fears that doctors habitually committed sane people to asylums. The advertisement, which poses as a news story under the title "Can Doctors Tell Insanity? Experience of the World's Reporter, Nellie Bly, Would Indicate Not"—warns that readers with "nervous troubles" might be at risk of "a terrible fate" if their symptoms are "mistaken for insanity."[53] Recapping Bly's revelations about Blackwell's Island, the "article" assures readers that Dr. Greene's Nervous Nerve Tonic can, if taken faithfully, protect the innocent. The exposé had become an item of intense interest and amusement—not to mention potential profit.[54]

By the time N. L. Munro published Bly's lightly edited articles as a book, the reporter had attempted to broaden the range of her sympathies. A brief introduction, which Bly signed, assures readers that "as a result of my visit to the asylum and the exposures consequent thereon, . . . the City of New York has appropriated $1,000,000 more than ever before for the care of the insane." The passages Bly (or her editors) added to the book version emphasize concern about standards of care, and they attempt to push the newspaper adventure story into something seemingly more sympathetic toward all mentally ill patients, not just "nervous cases," and possibly wrongly committed women. Near the beginning of the book, one new passage, for instance, suggests that Bly's intended purpose is to see if "the many stories of abuses in such institutions" have been "wildly exaggerated," the stuff of fictional "romances."[55]

If Bly's newspaper articles constitute yet another of those romances, the book alterations underscore the reality of the abuses. Bly extends more sympathetic commentary in the chapter "Promenading with Lunatics." Here, four additional paragraphs showcase her sentimental musings on what it must mean to be insane: "Mad! what can be half so horrible? My heart thrilled with pity when I looked on old, gray-haired women talking aimlessly to space. One woman had on a straight-jacket, and two women had to drag her along. Crippled, blind, old, young, homely, and pretty; one senseless mass of humanity. No fate could be worse." The beautiful landscape of Blackwell's Island, upon which virtually every journalistic visitor comments, seems only to mock the women:

> I looked at the pretty lawns, which I had once thought was such a comfort to the poor creatures confined on the Island, and laughed at my own notions. What enjoyment is it to them? They are not allowed on the grass—it is only to look at. I saw some patients eagerly and caressingly lift a nut or a colored leaf that had fallen on the path. But they were not permitted to keep them. The nurses would always compel them to throw their little bit of God's comfort away.
>
> As I passed a low pavilion, where a crowd of helpless lunatics were confined, I read a motto on the wall, "While I live I hope." The absurdity of it struck me forcibly. I would have liked to put above the gates that open to the asylum, "He who enters here leaveth hope behind."[56]

Bly's commentary here is at home with anything Fuller or Fern would write, and a final chapter in her book rounds out the revisions by detailing her appearance before a grand jury to testify about asylum conditions. This finale tempers the abrupt ending that concluded the original *World* articles. There, Bly, who was notoriously vain about her curly bangs, decides to forgo "risking [her] health—and her hair" by infiltrating the wards for more seriously ill and suicidal patients, and she returns triumphantly to her normal life.[57]

Though the additions for *Ten Days in a Mad-House* create a tone more sympathetic toward the mentally ill than the newspaper version, the added passages stand in tension with Bly's obvious concern: that sane women—or, at least, only "nervous" and therefore not really mentally ill women, in the thinking of many nineteenth-century Americans—have been wrongly committed and are endangered by the frightening maniacs, the mystifying psychotics, and the diabolical nurses and inept doctors who control them all. Bly did not remove any of these original points when she revised her work for *Ten Days in a Mad-House;* instead, she added eighty-three lines of text to the ninety-eight-page piece, along with the three-and-a-half-page final chapter about the grand jury, not nearly enough to remove the levity and adventurous flavor of the *World* articles, as epitomized by Bly's glib comment about her hair (one of several in the asylum work). The additions finally do little to shift the stereotyped drama of the story into a piece that incites the sympathies of readers into a project for institutional reform.

Other scholars have largely considered Bly's work in wholly muckraking terms, without exploring her positioning of herself within the text and certainly, in reading Bly's asylum articles critically, I do not mean to imply she possessed wholly mercenary motives. Clearly, asylum reform was necessary, and abuses abounded both on Blackwell's Island and at many other hospitals. At the end of the nineteenth century, basic conditions in many of America's public asylums had deteriorated to a shocking degree, and Edward Shorter points out that most institutions had by then "abandon[ed] any effort at therapy and had become, instead, public warehouses for undesirably ill people.[58] Where Fuller found much to admire about public asylums in the 1840s under the mantle of moral treatment, and Fern could praise patient care at the Blackwell's Island hospital in 1854, Bly's articles brought to light some of the pervasive emotional and physical abuses at the end of the century, and her reporting provoked serious investigation and increased funding for the institution. Nor do I wish to fault Bly for failing to show the same kind of sympathy that other newspaper women did when confronting mental illness. Bly tapped into broader public conversations about reform within a journalistic context that encouraged her to sensationalize that dialogue. Yet her reportage depended on a type of reportage that risked trivializing the most severe problems—and the sickest patients—at the asylum, and it may have functioned, in the end, as another form of asylum tourism. The New York Grand Jury investigated conditions at Blackwell's Island as a result of Bly's reporting, but in an era when the style of women's newspaper reporting was at least as important as the content, the question of whether or not sweeping reform was her goal remains open to debate.

More to the point, Bly did not *need* to convey the kind of sympathy evident in the other case studies I present—the kind of professional place she staked out for herself as a newspaper woman within the context of new journalism allowed her (perhaps even demanded she do so)—to shift the terms of the sympathetic story line. In securing professional territory, female reporters were no longer bound by a rhetoric of sympathy selflessly directed toward others and built on the foundations of female-centered sentimental fiction. This was, on the contrary, a journalism that made room for a new, strong figure to tell a dramatic tale of adventure, with the newspaper woman triumphing as the fearless, undaunted heroine.

Spectacles of Incarceration

The story of Nellie Bly's ten days in a madhouse was a spectacular success, and she sought fresh adventures and journalistic stunts to extend her professional reach. Just eighteen months after her madhouse debut, she performed undercover work at another public institution—this time a New York City jail—by posing as a robber and arranging for her own arrest. On the morning of February 24, 1889, some *New York World* readers must have been surprised to pick up their papers and read in large type, "Nellie Bly a Prisoner." Then again, perhaps no one was terribly surprised to discover, upon reading, that the arrest was another of Bly's amazing stunts, this one ostensibly involving an investigation of women's experiences in the city jail system. Her stated goals: to determine "how women—particularly innocent women—who fall into the hands of the police are treated by them," and to learn whether or not the city's jails need more female matrons.[59] Bly focuses her attention, in other words, not on the criminal class but on innocent women who have been arrested by mistake, an echo of her earlier concerns about women wrongfully held at the Blackwell's Island asylum.

At the article's beginning, Bly "goes incognito" in front of her own readers, describing first the confounding case of two women, Miss Kent and Miss Peters, who met on the train from Rochester to New York City. Mimicking the generic hallmarks of popular mystery fiction, this article explains that Miss Kent encouraged Miss Peters to stow her money in two different bags. Later, however, Miss Peters noticed that half of her cash was missing and called the police. Who stole Miss Peters's money, the reader wonders? Was it Miss Kent, as Miss Peters suspects? Or did Miss Peters simply lose the money and blame Miss Kent as a cover for her own carelessness? The charges against Miss Kent seem convincing. She had been left alone with one of Miss Peters's bags for some time, and now the money from that bag is gone. Miss Kent insists on her innocence, but police arrest her anyway and cart her to the station house. It is not until the article's second column that the reader learns, with relief, that "I—Nellie Bly—was Miss Kent, the girl who stood there accused of larceny."[60]

Bly proceeds to detail the various abuses and humiliations she faced in the city jail. She expresses shock, for instance, when guards recruit another prisoner to search her, for want of female matrons, and when a chink in the holding room wall allows men to peep as she undresses for the search. She is similarly appalled when a prison guard extends amorous advances. And she registers even more righteous indignation when a lawyer, a veritable wolf in attorney's clothing, attempts to trade his services for sexual favors, a seduction plot which the attractive and innocent maiden narrowly thwarts.

Bly's narrative stance bears striking resemblance to that of her madhouse articles. She, rather than the prison inmates, becomes the centrally cast actress in a manufactured drama that once again echoes the city-mystery fiction genre. Bly enacts the role of the naïve newcomer to the city, ignorant of the sinister urban underbelly, the heroine whose sexual purity appears at risk in the big bad world. With its focus on the newspaper woman, the article diverts attention toward the titillating details of her own adventure, rather than reportorial and readerly sympathy toward imprisoned women or questions about the desperate circumstances that have led them to jail, or even a consideration of whether their treatment is humane. The implication is that, while conditions in the jail are poor, normal prisoners—unlike the figure Bly represents—deserve their consequences.

Two incidents particularly illustrate this diversion of sympathetic identification. As a policeman leads Bly into the confines of the jail, she notices "a cell where a young man stood looking through the bars and a pale woman" who "leaned her face against the bars." As in Fern's prison pieces, readers observe the reporter as she, in turn, observes the prisoners. However, where Fern yearns to see past the prisoners' bars and through their eyes, thus grafting the prisoners' sad identities onto herself and readers, the other jailed women and men seem nearly ancillary in Bly's construction, supporting cast members in the drama. And where Fern's shifting gaze leads to fellow feeling, Bly's tends toward self-reference, reinforcing the sympathy and identification readers might extend to her as a modern newspaper woman, placed in the middle of an amazing story for their entertainment, rather than the prisoners, presumably locked up for actual crimes. The reporter places the prisoners and herself on display for the enormous *World* audience, but without the extension of emotional connection with the figures who share cell space with Bly, they remain potentially dangerous and certainly undesirable, a threat to the maiden's safety, in the literary framing of the text.

In similar fashion, Bly records with annoyance the sounds of drunken prisoners yelling incessantly for their release. Though irritated by the noise during her long night in jail, she expresses great amusement the next morning when the prisoners complain blearily about an early wakeup time: "It was very funny to hear the remarks of those who had been brought in dead drunk the night before," she notes, sardonically. Likewise, Bly blushes at the "foul," lurid remarks that female prisoners trade with their male jailors as they await a hearing before the judge. Indeed, "the women seemed to be having a contest to see who could say the most horrible things" as they banter with the men. "I have nothing to tell about it that could be published," she remarks, leaving it to her reader's own rich imagination to supply the naughty details.

The point seems clear: this public institution may be a place where the modern journalist can assert her professional voice, but it is no place for a proper woman. It threatens her womanhood and defiles her genteel status by displaying her before the less savory element of society. And since the journalist is in fact a proper woman, despite her atypical profession, Bly pictures herself standing apart from the real prisoners. As she draws attention to her difference from the lunatics in the madhouse articles, Bly registers her exceptional status in jail and positions herself as the deserving object of care. One guard offers her a cell near the stove. A turnkey brings a pillow and blanket to make her night in the jail more tolerable. The following morning, another guard orders for her a nourishing breakfast. The effect of these kindnesses is not to draw attention toward the prisoners—they, presumably, do not receive similar comforts—but to substantiate her own separation from them within the drama she has created. Ironically, the narrative framing also undermines any implicit complaint about innocent women locked up by mistake and therefore undermines Bly's implicit calls for reform. Judging from her experience, when innocent women are mistaken for criminals, they receive comparatively gentle treatment and speedy release.

At the end of her report on imprisonment as an innocent woman, Bly concludes that male guards are actually preferable over female because "women are never so kind to their unfortunate sisters as men are. Women grow harder from daily contact with crime, so that no sympathy is left in them." Bly's conclusion is curious, given the story's apparent aim to show the humiliations female prisoners undergo when male jailers examine and guard them—a direct contradiction to the reform-oriented plea for more prison matrons. Women like herself, she implies—*respectable* women who might find themselves falsely accused and unfairly incarcerated—require sympathy and reformed conditions. But she broadly hints that the lower-class women, who thirst for alcohol and banter profanely with prison guards—women, that is, whose own decisions have landed them in the slammer—do not require female matrons or improved physical conditions. Consequently, Bly limits her call for reform to a particular social class, one that presumably would not include a strong criminal element. As a result, her foray into the jail yields more entertainment for the voyeuristic newspaper consumer who seeks another variation on the familiar captivity narrative.[61]

Nellie Bly's popularity soared in large degree because, unlike Margaret Fuller, Fanny Fern, and Elizabeth Jordan, she did not push readers to confront their lack of sympathy for less privileged members of society. Instead, she gave audiences what they desired and what new journalism demanded of her as a new kind of journalist: confirmation of their own suspicions about madness and crime. As she performed the role of a newspaper woman who, quite literally, went places no female reporter had gone before, she broke trails through the city room for other women. However, the nature of new journalism dictated that the articles direct readers' sympathies (and, of course, their admiration) toward the intrepid female reporter who did things women were not "allowed" to do in real life and confirmed readers' suspicions about asylums and prisons in the process. Given Bly's job description, her stories thus materialize as narratives about the sympathy readers extended to her as a reporter rather than to prisoners and lunatics. They become, in some sense, about sympathetic *mis*-identification, a reworking of fellow feeling, reflecting the sensationalistic identity of late nineteenth-century urban journalism.[62]

I certainly do not wish to underestimate the impact Bly had in opening the door for other female journalists. As Jean Marie Lutes notes, her impersonations "allowed her to flaunt the very characteristics that were being used as an excuse to bar women from city newsrooms: her femaleness, her emotional expressiveness, her physical—even her explicitly sexual— vulnerability."[63] Stunt reporters like Bly could speak in the most public and influential medium of the time, and they marketed their professional mettle to justify their place on the city's Newspaper Row. Still, placing Bly's writing about asylums and prisons into conversation with those of other women in this study enriches the picture of how women used sympathy to bolster professional status—and how in the process they sometimes fulfilled readers' thirst for stereotypes about madness and crime, as well. As she dramatized herself, Bly crafted a different kind of sympathy, a sympathy of the marketplace.

CHAPTER 5

Sympathy and Sensation

Elizabeth Jordan, Lizzie Borden, and the Female Reporter in the Late Nineteenth Century

Write of things as they are, . . . and write of them as simply as you can.

—Elizabeth Jordan, *May Iverson's Career*

In 1889, Elizabeth Garver Jordan, an aspiring young woman from the Midwest, knocked on the door of John Cockerill, managing editor of the *New York World,* and bluntly asked for a job working in the newsroom. To her amazement, he hired her. Jordan proved her reportorial mettle in September of that year when she wrote her first "model story," titled "Tramped the Streets with a Corpse."[1] Despite the gruesome and sensationalistic headline, the piece told in simple, straightforward terms the sad tale of a mother who, abandoned by her husband and evicted by an indifferent mother-in-law, had wandered the cold city streets with her youngest child. "All night long [the mother] had tramped the streets with that tiny corpse," Jordan wrote, "wrapped in a ragged shawl, in her stiffened arms," only to discover the death when she lifted the shawl to feed the baby. The "wan-faced" woman fell into the nearest police station, where her baby was whisked away to the morgue and the mother given over to the Commissioners of Charities and Correction, a "prison," in the language of the article. Jordan's words moved her readers, but without raging sensationalism or maudlin prose. Rather, Jordan asked her readers to place themselves momentarily in the shoes of the grief-stricken mother, allowing the facts of the case to impart their own feeling. "Let your readers shed their own tears," Jordan had been advised by a mentor, a piece of advice she called the best "literary criticism I have ever received."[2] The story, which Jordan's editors held up as an exemplar of fine news writing, ushered her into the club of "regular fellow" male reporters, as she later remarked.

Women were still uncommon in the profession of newspaper journalism during the late nineteenth century, even though they established new professional roles, as exemplified by Nellie Bly, and their ranks swelled in the final two decades of the century—in 1880 only 288 women were reporters or editors, a number that shot up to 600 just ten years later.[3] Still, they occupied a tenuous position. In an era that still considered "hard news" within mass-market newspapers as decided masculine territory, built as it was on bearing witness to the darkest realities of the city, women struggled to claim space for themselves against attitudes that argued the newsroom would ruin the femininity of any self-respecting female. Women in the newsroom, the place Ishbel Ross, an early historian of women's journalism, called "that sound haunt of masculinity" in the late nineteenth century, continued to face obstructive skepticism from their male colleagues, many of whom were convinced that "women were only capable of fluff or tear-jerking stories."[4] But both in her reporting and in her fiction about reporting, Jordan turned that "feminine" tendency toward emotion and sympathy—liabilities in the minds of male reporters—into rhetorical assets. Ultimately, she argued, the female reporter was particularly equipped to produce more realistic and "objective" writing, and she did so, paradoxically, by calling on a sense of sympathy for the newspaper subject.[5] In the process, she encouraged readers to question and complicate their reactions to the subjects of her article, including their reactions to one of the most important criminal trials of the century: that of Lizzie Borden.

Jordan, one of the most prolific reporters, authors, and editors of her time, stands as a notable example of how women drew on a rhetoric of sympathy as a strategy for positioning themselves in the changing newspaper profession and the broader literary marketplace of the late nineteenth century. In her wide-ranging career as a journalist, fiction writer, playwright, and editor, Jordan's work reached countless readers and fellow authors, and scholars have only begun to pay attention to her work editing *Harper's Bazar* and cowriting composite novels.[6] Her work as a newspaper reporter for Pulitzer's *New York World*, though, remains under-explored. Jordan's position on the *World* coincided with the advent of her fiction-writing career, and an examination of her newspaper stories alongside some of her fictional works—many of which are "newspaper fictions," or stories that take as their central topic the life of a reporter—underscores the dramatic interplay between fiction and reportage that influenced both fields in the late nineteenth century. Moreover, the comparison illuminates how Jordan carved a space for herself as a professional by using the language of female sympathy, even against the constraints of a rising aesthetic of masculinized realism.

This chapter considers one of Jordan's earliest newspaper fictions—a tale about reporter Ruth Herrick, who trumps her male colleagues by interviewing a female murder suspect—and places it alongside her own newspaper coverage of a curiously similar murder case, that of the infamous Lizzie Borden. Read together, these works articulate a rhetoric of sympathy for the incarcerated woman, which Jordan manipulates to situate the figure of the newspaper woman in the literary and journalistic marketplaces of the late nineteenth century. The story and articles call for a sympathetic, yet paradoxically "objective," reading of the murder suspect, and they locate the ability to sympathize in the figure of the female reporter, who possesses the skill to affect readers and uncover what nineteenth-century Americans called "the real thing," the truth behind the news story.

"Emotional" Women in the Late Nineteenth-Century Newsroom

While reporters like Bly and Jordan longed to be taken seriously as journalists, even under the more hospitable mantle of new journalism, stereotypes still depicted women as overly emotional, thereby undercutting their authority as sources of balance, truthfulness, and realism, the bedrocks of what would in the early twentieth century be called "journalistic objectivity." As Kathleen Cairns notes, some women found employment in the late nineteenth century and early twentieth century by embracing that stereotype quite literally and writing "stories that would wring tears of sorrow and sympathy from readers."[7] By the early twentieth century, that type of explicitly gendered reporting had suffered a fatal backlash from critics and readers, who condemned such compositions as careless and manipulative "sob sister" reportage. However, in the late nineteenth century, Jordan turned back on itself the idea that women's natural sympathy unsuited them to work in a tough "man's job." She self-consciously appropriated the voice of sympathy and highlighted it, arguing that it was, ironically, the key to finding the reality behind the news lead.

Men who opposed hiring female journalists in the late nineteenth century feared that emotionally laden women were unable to compose the news with the required realistic lens. Critics positioned realism, as a literary construct, within masculine terms, and it was a style increasingly suspicious of emotion.[8] Writers had of course demonstrated a dedication to authenticity throughout the century, as evidenced by Fuller's and Fern's writing—the types of texts Daniel Borus calls "protorealism." Nevertheless, the realists characterized themselves as breaking with other literary forms, specifically sentimentality, turning the novelist into an "unattached observer" who "convert[ed] the stuff of life into fiction" and examined "the world dispassionately, as if it were under a microscope."[9] Facts would therefore, in Henry James's words, "catch the colour, the relief, the expression, the surface, the substance of the human spectacle."[10]

Realism had its critics, of course. Opponents believed literature should deal primarily in uplifting and moral topics. Realism, conversely, "crowd[ed] the world of fiction with commonplace people; people whom one would positively avoid coming into contact with in real life," as one late nineteenth-century critic complained.[11] Howells, a central proponent of realism, shocked many of his readers when he rejected writing about "fundamental and eternal beliefs about God, man, and society" in favor of more frank discussion of social issues.[12] Realist writers associated "women's writing," in turn, with other segments of the literary marketplace, particularly popular sentimental novels, which, as earlier in the century, retained their connection with emotionality. Mainstream literary history argues that literary realism came to define the marketplace in the late nineteenth century, but as June Howard points out, while "prestigious writing . . . became less openly emotional and more ambitiously intellectual, less directly didactic and more conspicuously masculine," sentimental literature still played a significant—even dominant—role in the literary marketplace. Indeed, sentimental and romantic literature, with "its legitimizing conventions and capacity for engendering solidarities," ensured its importance in the late nineteenth century, especially for "writers with minimal print access."[13] The debate about sentimental versus realist texts became as well a debate about highbrow and lowbrow culture, and about gender itself. As Michael Davitt Bell contends, in the late nineteenth century men "project[ed] their anxieties" about authorship "onto women," and "literary historians have often associated such anxiety in the second half of the nineteenth century with the conversion of high art into a more rigidly masculine field that would escape the 'contaminating' effects of women." Realism "sought to ally itself with 'the world of men's activities.'" Presuming that women had no understanding of the starkest realities of life and were ruled by emotion over dispassion, realists "in effect prohibited women from full participation on the realist program," though they found expression for realism, notably in "local color" fiction.[14]

In light of the gendered tensions inherent in the interplay between realist fiction and the newspaper industry, Jordan's task—indeed, the task of any female journalist seeking to navigate the newsroom—was to turn her "liability," that is, her "natural" female emotionality, into a rhetoric that upended the emerging ideals of masculine realism and "objectivity." A distinction is necessary here, however, between the kind of sympathy Jordan exuded toward her fictional characters, the actual figure of Lizzie Borden, and the overwrought sentimentality that later characterized female reporting in the effusive sob sister narratives of the early twentieth century, which introduced only the most marketable kind of sympathy, as I discuss briefly in my afterword and which, I maintain, dominates some of Bly's best-known work. Jordan aimed for a more nuanced brand of emotion. She called on her readers to use the kind of *critical* sympathy, exhibited as well by Fuller and Fern, a deeper consideration of the murder suspect predicated on the desire to understand her rather than to profit by her. She gently allowed her readers to shed private tears and thereby develop sympathy for the subject of the news story, whether or not she was guilty. In essence, echoing Fuller, she asked her readers to approach such women as Lizzie Borden as they would characters in a skillfully drawn fiction—not one involving stock villains and heroines, but one with a more complex and ambiguous cast. Jordan implicitly mocked overwrought emotion in her 1902 fiction collection *Tales of Destiny*. Miss Underhill, a sardonic, sarcastic reporter for the fictional *New York Searchlight* scoffs at "teary tales," or "news stories full of sadness" until she eventually discovers, through Jordan's wry and ironic voice, the marketable power of stories that make "New York [weep]."[15] This kind of superficial sympathetic identification sold papers and earned women a place in the newsroom, but Jordan ultimately rejected it as insincere—not "real."

Sympathy in Newspaper Fiction:
Elizabeth Jordan and Meta-Narrative

Born in Milwaukee in 1865, Jordan began writing seriously as a schoolgirl. While she believed, upon her high school graduation, that her future awaited her in a convent, her mother pushed for a musical education. Her father devised a compromise: his daughter would go into newspaper work as an "apprenticeship" for a career in literature. Jordan's first job was editing the women's page for *Peck's Sun* in Milwaukee, a limiting position that she disliked. Coveting an environment that would allow her to cover hard news, she descended upon New York and Pulitzer's *World*. "Progress," she once remarked, "meant one thing only": a "place on the *New York World's* staff," a job she held for ten years, until leaving to become the editor of *Harper's Bazar*.[16]

Jordan began work for the *World* in the summer of 1889 in a most conventional sense, composing a social column, "The Season of Outing," a type of journalism she found "shock[ing] and humiliat[ing]," and certainly not much better than the work she had performed in Milwaukee. She was forced to pen puff pieces "about Long Island summer resorts, articles frankly designed to please hotel proprietors and stimulate advertising, local pride, and *World* circulation," Jordan recounted in her insightful 1938 memoir, *Three Rousing Cheers*. Despite the tedium of the assignment, Jordan kept her society-reporter job and watched for her big break, which arrived, conveniently enough, on the seashore, when she scooped numerous male reporters who had been unsuccessful in describing President Benjamin Harrison's vacation days at Cape May, New Jersey. Arriving at the Harrison home unannounced, Jordan formed an immediate connection with the first lady, procured the story about the presidential family on vacation, and burst open the professional doors that had blocked her way. As she put it, Mrs. Harrison "had no knowledge that she was starting me out on a new life. . . . I built a shrine for her in that hour, and I have kept a little candle burning there throughout my life."[17] Jordan indeed owed much to the Harrison story on the strength of her scoop: she received a handsome job promotion and started to receive assignments that moved her out of the parlor of the women's pages and into the city room on Manhattan's Newspaper Row.[18]

Jordan's popularity grew with a regular column called "True Stories of the News," half-page daily pieces that, she explained, "were to be taken from the daily happenings in New York—those bits of drama which are often covered by a few lines in a newspaper," such as "the finding of an unknown body in the river; the suicide of an unknown girl; some pregnant incident in the prisons or courtrooms or hospitals of the big city." Her job "was to dig up all the facts back of the news leads and write each story as fiction, hung on its news hook."[19] Ross writes that Jordan "combined the best features of the stunt age with sound writing. She tested the accommodations of jails and asylums, rode an engine cab, interviewed social leaders and covered the news of the town.... She visited a lonely mining camp in the mountains, in which no woman had ever set foot. Armed with a Spanish stiletto she explored the camps of the moonshiners and did a series for the Sunday *World* that was copied widely."[20] Although most of these articles were published without a byline, newspaper editors sometimes indicated that the writer was one of their intrepid female reporters. For instance, a short column about the women's section of the Tombs, part of a larger article about the infamous prison, includes an image of a female reporter— possibly Jordan herself—"taking a prisoner's story" (see fig. 8).[21]

IN THE FEMALE PRISON.

Stories of Innocence and Crime from the Feminine Prisoners.

The social atmosphere in the female prison of the Tombs is at times something not to be despised. Unlike the men, the women are allowed their freedom, and they wander about, visiting, chatting and comparing fancy work, with as little restraint as if they were only paying patients in a fashionable sanitarium.

TAKING A PRISONER'S STORY.

The woman's prison is square, one end meeting the wall and the three tiers on the three sides. On the first floor is the big stove around which gather the poor creatures in striped gowns and tawdry finery that represent the drunken, disorderly unfortunate who continually drift in and out. Here these women huddle together on the benches and settle the affairs of their world. On the stove they cook many a contraband potato and brew many a can of tea, their spirits apparently not a whit disturbed. Now and

Figure 8. The *New York World* highlighted the role of newspaper women as they gathered hard news, rather than writing the typical soft news about "women's issues." An article about the Tombs, for instance, includes an image of a female reporter "taking a prisoner's story" ("Voices from the Tombs," *New York World*, November 24, 1889; University of Arkansas Libraries, Fayetteville)

Like Bly, Jordan enjoyed a gift for drafting the dramatic, human interest stories favored by readers of new journalism, stories that blurred the lines between fiction and news, and it wasn't long before she began writing straight fiction inspired by her news stories. Since Bly and Jordan were on the *World*'s payroll at the same time, their paths inevitably crossed, though they were not particularly friendly. Jordan admitted in her memoir that, upon meeting Bly, she told the older woman that she meant "to confine myself to news reporting," as opposed to stunt-making.[22] Jordan's comment likely had much to do with Bly's chilly reception. Her first book of short stories, composed in the early 1890s and collected in 1898 under the title *Tales of the City Room*, depicted the work of newspaper women and "influenced many women to work as journalists."[23] The introductory story in this collection, "Ruth Herrick's Assignment," most fully portrays how the female journalist uses a framework of sympathy toward an accused murderer in her quest for the reality behind the news item. The story also provides a fitting backdrop for a reading of how Jordan used similar fictional constructs in framing the sensational trial of Lizzie Borden in 1893.

"Ruth Herrick's Assignment" is written in the mode of the "newspaper tale" or "newspaper fiction," a successful subgenre at the turn of the century, popularized in part by such authors as Richard Harding Davis and Jordan. Meta-textual in nature, newspaper fiction depicts the work of reporters and newsboys, characters whose gruff exteriors have been hardened by fearless pursuit of "the real thing"—hard news. With plots frequently drawn from the actual scenarios and stories reporters had encountered on the job, the genre provided readers an entertaining insider's view of life in the newsroom. As a popular form, newspaper fiction dramatized the news-making experience by casting the reporter as the hero of both the newsroom and the city's streets and providing readers with a provocative insider's view of the romance and rigor of reporting. "True Stories of the News" built on the conventions of early newspaper fiction, just as newspaper fiction built on the conventions of articles like those that appeared in "True Stories of the News." Despite the gritty realism depicted in such stories, newspaper fiction also featured emotionally touching moments, for the protagonist ultimately "behaves in the most sentimental fashion, all for the love of the paper."[24] Such tales, resting (as realist fiction often did itself) in a liminal space between newspaper articles and purely imaginative writing, enjoyed notable success in the literary marketplace of late nineteenth-century

America. If meta-fiction entails writing about writing itself, newspaper fictions layered meta-fiction atop meta-journalism, chronicling the arduous and adventurous path reporters take to gather and compose the news.

The title character of "Ruth Herrick's Assignment" is a young star reporter for the *New York Searchlight,* whose editor sends her to a local jail to interview one Helen Brandow, who awaits trial on the charge that she murdered her wealthy husband. Other reporters (by implication, all male) have clamored unsuccessfully to interview Mrs. Brandow, and now the coveted opportunity is about to drop in Herrick's lap. It is sure to be a "big beat," an "important exclusive story" that will assure the success of Herrick's paper and her career as well. A "beat," the narrator explains, is a "story which only one newspaper gets, and which all the other newspapers wanted. A reporter with the right spirit will move heaven and earth to get it for the journal he represents." Herrick possesses the "right spirit," but the subject of this "beat" is inscrutable; she "has not spoken a word since her arrest." As such, Herrick's job description is simple: "It is your business to make her talk," her editor informs her. "Interview her and write the best story you ever wrote in your life. . . . If you are ambitious, here is your chance to distinguish yourself."[25]

Herrick is indeed ambitious, and she takes up the challenge with gusto, though the prisoner initially refuses to share any information. As the women converse, however, a sense of sympathy flowers between them. Bit by bit, Mrs. Brandow paints a picture of her unhappy marriage until, quite unexpectedly, she confesses that she did, indeed, murder her husband, driven to that act by his violence. Herrick now possesses the single piece of information that the rest of the city's reporters have struggled in vain to uncover—that Helen Brandow is guilty. If Herrick can report this sensational news in the *Searchlight,* her "beat" is made, and her career along with it.

If this were a typical newspaper fiction, Herrick would naturally fulfill that beat, given her ambition and the money-making potential for her paper. But in asserting the superior news-gathering ability of the female journalist, Jordan upends some of the conventions of the newspaper fiction genre—not to mention expectations about good reporting. Hearing Mrs. Brandow's sad tale rouses Herrick's emotion, one of the marks of a good reporter. While she is "usually a cool, unemotional young person," knowledge of the murder "profoundly move[s]" her and awakens a sense of sympathy for the accused woman. Herrick's heart and mind struggle in a battle between sympathetic identification and professional ambition. She has obtained what she sought at the jail—the real story of Mrs. Brandow—and "now she [has] the 'biggest beat' of the year" for her paper. Herrick envisions the "commotion in the managing editor's office when the news" of success arrives, and she anticipates his pleasure over her professional skill.[26] Still, despite the golden path opening before her eyes, she hesitates, moved by the woman sitting before her and by a conviction that the more complex truth of the story—the "real thing" she seeks as a good reporter—lies beyond the simple fact (and sensation) of Mrs. Brandow's technical guilt.

Herrick realizes that Mrs. Brandow is a noble woman who has been driven to a desperate act by an abusive husband, and now this journalistic "beat" will lead to her life-long imprisonment. Herrick struggles with an agonizing decision: "If anything but the life of a human being had been at stake, how proudly and gladly she would have gone to [her editor], and how hard she would have tried to write the best story of her life, as he had ordered. But—this other woman at her feet. Something within the reporter asserted itself as counsel for her and pleaded and would not [back] down."[27] The pleading voice comes, specifically, out of her sympathy for the other woman, a gendered language that passes subliminally between Mrs. Brandow and Ruth Herrick, and this sympathy leads to a richer comprehension of the murderer's story. In a plot development similar to one imagined by Susan Glaspell some two decades later in her play *Trifles* and short story "A Jury of Her Peers," Herrick becomes the private judge and jury for Mrs. Brandow, weighing the evidence before her and handing down the verdict on a woman who has been driven to murder her own husband.

Unlike Glaspell's story, however, this one adds the weight of Herrick's professional ambitions, and her deliberations are far more personal. On the one hand, she sees the fate of Mrs. Brandow, should Herrick publish this confession. Even if Mrs. Brandow does not receive a death sentence, a dismal prison life stretches before her. On the other hand, if Herrick silences herself and refuses to publish the confession, she might jeopardize her career and undermine her paper. Herrick is in a tight spot, faced with the possibility that "she, the practical; she, the loyal; she was going to allow her paper to be 'thrown down' on the biggest story of the year!" Yet, finally, that is what Herrick allows to happen, driven to her decision by the refrain of "one more chance" for Helen Brandow, running through her mind. To resolve the conflict, she tells Mrs. Brandow she will kill the story, provided the accused woman will not grant interviews to any other reporter, for "he might be more loyal [to his paper] than I."[28]

Herrick's reference to the male reporter here is telling, for in her story, Jordan distinguishes between the efforts of men and those of the female reporter. The public has known only the picture of Mrs. Brandow drawn by male reporters. "Newspaper men," the reader learns, "had been gushing in their descriptions of the famous prisoner, possibly because their imaginations were stimulated by the fact that many of them had never seen her."[29] Male reporters write Mrs. Brandow into existence based on their own sensation-hungry assumptions—assumptions that misinterpret both the woman and the story. The men have failed to compose an "objective" story; they have not witnessed the suspect firsthand, as Herrick has. It is their writing, not the female reporter's, which is flawed and lacking in reality. The men produce a story for their newspapers, but it is up to the female reporter to get the *correct* story, an echo of Bly's refrain in the asylum articles. And so it is Ruth Herrick who has the chance to expose Mrs. Brandow; she has been able to see the true woman precisely because of her ability to sympathize with the accused murderer. If readers wish to read the most "objective" and truthful news, the story argues, they must determine who possesses genuine sympathy: the reporter who finds the private truth lying behind the public facade of the subject. The illustrations that accompany the story in its original publication context in *Cosmopolitan* magazine emphasize this moment of genuine sympathy, portraying the imprisoned woman weeping before the newspaper woman as she struggles with the dilemma placed before her (see fig. 9).

The dramatic irony, of course, is that because of this sympathy, if she is to save the other woman from a presumably undeserved fate, Herrick cannot publish her interview with Mrs. Brandow. And so she kills her own story. At the end of the tale, her editor expresses disappointment that his unflappable reporter has not obtained any fresh information from the interview with Mrs. Brandow. Her "failure" seems to confirm his own prejudices, and he concludes, "After all, you can't depend on a woman in this business."[30] The joke, of course, is on the editor. What he fails to realize is that female sympathy has uncovered the real story—but that sympathy has also rendered Ruth Herrick silent. If newspaper women, in general,

Figure 9. The original publication of "Ruth Herrick's Assignment" in *Cosmopolitan* magazine (July 1894) included images that emphasized the sympathetic tie between the newspaper woman and the accused murderer. (Author's collection)

insist on amplifying their public voices, Herrick quells hers here, but she does so because of her own gendered sense of professional superiority. She refuses to divulge the story to her editor and newspaper readers, and so she cannot display her exemplary reporting skills. But Jordan, as fiction writer, does share the secret with the short story audience. On the surface it would appear that the piece confirms male fears that, because of their emotion and sympathy, female journalists cannot be trusted to produce good journalism. Jordan turns those fears upside down and leaves no doubt as to who is the better reporter and who has access to "the real," precisely because she holds fellow feeling as a higher law. Sympathy and "objectivity" are linked finally to the female reporter, working—and prevailing—in a man's business.[31]

LIFE MIRRORS ART:
FRAMING THE CASE OF LIZZIE BORDEN

When, in 1893, about a year after writing "Ruth Herrick's Assignment," Elizabeth Jordan composed another story about a woman accused of murder, she drew on an ethos of sympathy to suggest once again that her reporting about the accused woman was the most reliable, "objective," and true account, and this time she presented that narrative within the pages of the *New York World*. Like Mrs. Brandow in "Ruth Herrick's Assignment," Lizzie Borden had been accused of murdering a close family member—two, in fact, her father and stepmother—and exposing the arguably pathologically domestic space of the Bordens to the public eye. The evidence against Borden seemed overwhelming. Andrew and Abby Borden, of Fall River, Massachusetts, had each been struck with an ax in the head on a sweltering mid-morning in August 1892, within their own locked home, if not the forty and forty-one times of nursery-rhyme lore, then at least repeatedly enough to obliterate their features. While the family's maid was in her garret bedroom, ill from the three-day-old mutton the household had consumed for breakfast, Lizzie discovered her father's corpse and directed investigators to her stepmother's body, though she was disconcertingly vague about her own whereabouts that morning.

Like Mrs. Brandow, Borden was inscrutable, refusing to speak to reporters or defend herself publicly. As a result, many articles originally depicted her as a cold, unfeeling monster, and when Jordan covered the Borden trial for the *World* she noticed widespread condemnation bubbling within the courthouse, largely from other townswomen. Drawing on some of the same sentimental themes used in "Ruth Herrick's Assignment," Jordan framed the story of Lizzie Borden by asking her audience to read the accused woman with more sympathy than previous news reports had made possible and to explore Borden's character more carefully. In the process, Jordan argued implicitly that her own coverage was closer to the actual story of Lizzie Borden than that of articles in other newspapers, which offered superficial and sensationalistic pictures of a possible monster.[32]

Jordan's articles about the Borden trial, like those of competing journalists, include lengthy excerpts quoted directly from the trial transcripts. Typically, they set the scene for the day's testimony and provide a blow-by-blow of the testimony, with the reporter's occasional contextualizing thrown in. Jordan's articles, however, include a distinctive narrative subtext, a critical exploration of gendered sympathy, as filtered through the newspaper woman. Throughout her work, Jordan explores the debate about whether Borden is guilty of murdering her father and stepmother, but she also weaves in the tale of how other women react to the trial. Through this secondary story, Jordan registers her own careful sympathy as a female journalist, a trait testifying to superior reporting—she is able to read the true nature of Lizzie Borden, while male reporters and the women in the courtroom who refuse to show public sympathy cannot because they have been influenced by bad journalism, which has asked them to gaze on and consume the incarcerated female merely as an object for their own entertainment. If newspaper editors viewed women as principal consumers, here Jordan questions that consumption when the accused female criminal is fighting for her life. And she builds the framing artfully, crafting her factual stories for the *World* so they resemble the style of her own newspaper fiction.

Sympathy emerges as a narrative subtext in almost every article Jordan filed during the two-week-long trial.[33] However, one column she wrote near the end of the trial is particularly cogent in its positioning of the female journalist as the embodiment of sympathy toward the accused woman. "This Is the Real Lizzie Borden" was billed in a sub-headline as "A pen picture and character study of the most interesting woman of the week"; moreover, the article includes Jordan's byline, not a common practice even in the 1890s. This "pen picture," then, decisively originates from a woman scrutinizing another woman and, in turn, scrutinizing other women in the courtroom as they, too, scrutinize Borden. The overriding point of the text is that other, male-authored news reports have misrepresented Borden. Jordan, though, emerges as the reporter especially qualified to clarify the character in question, much as Ruth Herrick does in Jordan's short story, precisely because she is a newspaper woman.

Jordan begins with the same premise she poses in "Ruth Herrick's Assignment." Two Lizzie Bordens exist, just as do two Helen Brandows: one created by the male-dominated press, the other rightfully identified by the sympathizing female reporter, who is able to gain access to her fellow woman and thereby discern actuality behind the facade of the story. One of these Bordens is "the very wretched woman who is now on trial for her life in the little courthouse at New Bedford, Mass.," while the "other is a journalistic creation, skillfully built up by correspondents and persistently dangled before the eyes of the American people." This "journalistic creation" is false, for Borden has been portrayed as a "human sphinx, a thing without heart or soul. . . . It deserves no sympathy and receives none. This is the Lizzie Borden of the press."[34] Like Mrs. Brandow, Borden has been falsely depicted by the predominantly male press, and that false depiction has swayed other reporters and readers. Out of their own negative emotions, they are already moved to convict Borden; they are incapable of reading her character and story both with sympathy and, coincidentally, with "objectivity."

Jordan, of course, presents yet another journalistic creation of Lizzie Borden, but this time, she implies, her position—her ability as a woman to sympathize with the female murder suspect and thus read her character more thoroughly—allows her to give readers the real story. She digs past the fictions that make other journalists' work suspect. Her reporting, she promises, is the creation of a female writer who has intimately studied Borden's "face, nature, and character."[35] And intimate she is. Jordan minutely describes Borden's clothing and features. She counts the dental fillings in Borden's mouth. She catalogues each glimmer of emotion that passes over her face. She notices the soles of her shoes. She reads, in short, the evidence of Lizzie Borden's own body, and the implication is clear: You can trust me, for I have access to the actual Lizzie Borden. I am the objective observer of this woman, and I am also sympathetic to the plight of the accused, whether or not she is guilty. As Fuller and Fern do when they place themselves into their own scenes in order to warn against objectifying criminals, Jordan characterizes herself as the best reader of Lizzie Borden. In that closeness, we see as sympathetic a portrayal of the accused murderer as Ruth Herrick offers to Mrs. Brandow in "Ruth Herrick's Assignment."

Jordan's sympathy also emerges in contrast to the disdain shown by the other women present in the courtroom. Jordan notes that Borden stands alone at the bar, abandoned by female friends, for the women attending the trial stand almost universally opposed to Borden. Behind the rows of newspaper correspondents, Jordan says, and "filling every available inch of space and banked against the walls like an exhibit of poppies and dahlias at a flower show, sit the wives and mothers and maiden ladies of Fall River and New Bedford," women "untrammeled by logic and unmoved by sympathy," women who "judge and gloat."[36] One of the illustrations accompanying Jordan's work captures the gloating as it depicts a group of these women, clustered together in the courtroom and declaring their surety in Borden's guilt (fig. 10). These women judge Borden as readily as the jury of twelve men, but this casual jury has already reached its verdict, helped along by the false picture of Borden they have read in the newspaper, formed by the male journalists whom Jordan inventories in her description of the courtroom. This is what the journalistic accounts of others have created—the courtroom women believe Borden is guilty because the newspapers have persuaded them that her calm, dispassionate exterior masks a murderous rage. The women, however, have swallowed a false, sensationalistic story, and the female reporter has arrived to set her fellow women—and the rest of her readers—straight, to expose the fallacy of the earlier stories and critique their public stance against Borden, just as Ruth Herrick has the opportunity to educate her readers regarding the true nature of Mrs. Brandow. Jordan aims, that is, to transform the private sympathies of her readers so that their public attitudes might change.

Jordan's articles demonstrate her concern about the courtroom observers' abilities to see as clearly as she—and hopefully her readers—can. The women in the courtroom have been blinded not by excessive sympathy but by lack of it. Jordan repeatedly notes how many women clamor for admittance to the trial each day. She is dismayed by their sheer excitement at the prospect that one of their own sex might be found guilty of the heinous murders and condemned to prison for life; another illustration in the *World* depicts Jordan interviewing these overexcited women as they share their rather sanguinary opinions (fig. 11). These spectators have shown up to consume the sensational news—indeed, to consume the accused murderer—and Jordan's disapproving voice pervades her descriptions of them. For instance, one day Borden faints in court, and Jordan notes that "there were twenty-five women in the court-room, one of them sitting within the bar but a few feet away, yet not one of them came to [Borden's] assistance."[37]

The women in the courtroom have failed their sex because of their inattention to Borden as an actual person rather than a spectacle, and Jordan is appalled that inside and outside the courtroom they comfortably bask in the vacuous excitement surrounding Borden, thirsting for the most sensationalistic news accounts. In "Ruth Herrick's Assignment," Mrs. Brandow notes that the women of the prison town all crowd and gawk at her when she moves between the prison and the courthouse. "When I have been escorted back and forth they have been suspended over picket-fences watching me go by," Mrs. Brandow relates to Herrick.[38] Similarly, Jordan depicts the

Figure 10. An illustrator for the *New York World* accompanied Elizabeth Jordan as she sought the material for her "pen pictures," adding literal pen pictures that reinforced Jordan's writing about the gossiping, critical women who attended Lizzie Borden's trial (June 18, 1893). (University of Minnesota Libraries, Minneapolis)

TALKING IT OVER WITH THE REPORTER

Figure 11. One *New York World* image (June 18, 1893) placed Jordan at the center of newsgathering as she interviewed female spectators gathered at the Lizzie Borden trial. (University of Minnesota Libraries, Minneapolis)

crowds of women who gather outside the New Bedford courthouse hoping to catch a glimpse of the infamous woman. "The pressure of the crowd around the gateway at critical hours is something fearful," Jordan notes. "The worst of it is that the crowd is almost entirely composed of women and young girls." This crowd displays an "overmastering curiosity to catch even so much as a glance at Lizzie Borden." For three blocks, the streets are packed with people—80 percent of them women and girls—waiting to see Lizzie. It looks like "a country street down which a circus procession was expected to pass"—a spectacle of alleged criminality, passing itself off as circuslike entertainment.[39] These women swarm the courthouse every day, clamoring to gain entry. Opening the courthouse doors in the morning is akin to opening floodgates.

Jordan emphatically distrusts this voyeurism, and she offers her readers something born, instead, out of sympathy for the accused murderer— an ability to read Borden personally and read also the nuances of her case—and, perhaps paradoxically, out of an "objectivity" that prevents the newspaper audience from reaching a misinformed conclusion before the end of the trial. She seeks, that is, a counterbalance to the kind of overly sensationalistic journalism that has encouraged the women inside and outside the courthouse to condemn Borden so casually. To strike this journalistic balance and merge it with the ideal of sympathy, Jordan borrows the narrative framework of the mystery tale. She poses the case as an inexplicable mystery that could turn either way on the question of Borden's innocence or guilt, repeatedly insisting that the trial could end as easily in a guilty verdict as one of innocence (much as she dramatizes the case of Helen Brandow as capable of going either way). In one article, for instance, she writes that "all that Borden has done or said is equally consistent with the theory of innocence or the theory of guilt."[40] Similarly, in another article she notes, "It is a curious thing about this most mysterious and contradictory case that there is nothing so far in actual evidence that Miss Borden has said or done that is not consistent with the theory of her guilt or her innocence."[41]

Is Lizzie Borden guilty or innocent? The evidence points in both directions, and Jordan merely asks her readers to approach the matter critically, an act that requires a degree of sympathy and an ability to avoid prejudging Borden based on town gossip and the incomplete stories offered by other reporters. The case is a contradictory, confused mess, with points that could sway the jury toward either innocence or guilt, and the good writer will influence the good, sympathetic reader to suspend judgment until the accused woman projects her own voice. Using this narrative device, of course, heightens the suspense of the story and adds to the dramatic journalism that readers in the late nineteenth century expected in their newspapers. But the framing also signals another way Jordan's articles more directly echo the tenor of her earlier short story: Jordan seems to feel the responsibility greatly. Remaining duty-bound to her position as a reporter of "straight news," as she described her journalistic style, she nevertheless feels compelled to turn a sympathetic eye toward the accused "criminal" as she composes her stories, so that a public too easily swayed by dramatic conclusions might pause to consider the nuances of the case, much the way that a reader of Jordan's fictional newspaper story would accept the idea that a woman might be both guilty and innocent of the same crime.[42]

HELEN BRANDOW MEETS LIZZIE BORDEN

Jordan reads the female murder suspect with sympathy, and the female reporter fills the role of responsible sympathizer in both the newspaper fiction Jordan wrote and in the reports she filed from Borden's trial. Jordan's assertions about the factuality of her own sympathetic reporting seemed justified when Borden was acquitted for the murders of her father and step-mother in June 1893. After the trial, however, public opinion increasingly argued that Borden had been wrongly acquitted, and because of the way Jordan depicted her in her news stories, controversy arose when "Ruth Herrick's Assignment" was published for the first time in *Cosmopolitan* magazine in July 1894, one year after Borden's acquittal. Jordan contended that she had written the story well before the trial, but because of the sympathetic tones shown in both the newspaper tale and the actual newspaper reports, some readers believed she possessed secret knowledge of Borden's guilt, which she had suppressed in her own reporting. In her words, "it was immediately suggested and then generally assumed that Lizzie Borden had confessed her guilt to me, and that I had let her off"—not a surprising conclusion for an audience to make, though Jordan insisted she wrote the story before the trial.[43]

Compelled to address the controversy brought about by the curious intersection of "Ruth Herrick's Assignment" and her coverage of the Borden trial, Jordan returned to the case of Helen Brandow once again during her career as a novel writer, in another newspaper fiction clearly influenced by her experience with Borden. In 1914 she published one of her popular series of "May Iverson" books—*May Iverson's Career*—in which she describes Iverson as a newspaper reporter for the *New York Searchlight*, the same fictional newspaper for which the character Ruth Herrick writes. In one of the book's episodes, Jordan reworks the story of the Helen Brandow case, and this time her meta-textual play grows even more self-referential. May Iverson's editor calls on his ambitious reporter (another Jordan alter ego) to interview Helen Brandow as she awaits the conclusion of her trial for the murder of her husband. As in "Ruth Herrick's Assignment," male reporters have failed to coax Mrs. Brandow into interviews, but Iverson protests to her editor that she should not be the one to beg for an interview; the young reporter fears she cannot be a fair journalist since she has already reached a conclusion about the woman's innocence and could not be sufficiently "objective." Nevertheless, Iverson agrees to interview the accused woman, or at least to obtain a description of her jail cell. "Leave mawkish sympathy out of it," her editor instructs her. "Show her as she is—a murderess whose trial is going to make American justice look like a hole in a doughnut."[44] Unlike the newspaper women, the male editor lacks sympathy and, by implication, "objectivity" as well.

As she leaves the office, Iverson jokes that she is going to make Brandow "confess to me," and "then we'll suppress the confession!" In a curious bit of roman á clef, Jordan incorporates her own experiences with both the fictional Helen Brandow and the factual Lizzie Borden: she fictionalizes herself in May Iverson, pretending to write the story of how she wrote not only the stories of Helen Brandow/Lizzie Borden but those of "Ruth Herrick's Assignment" as well. She tells the story of the conflict itself, dramatizing the real-life scandal that arose when her own newspaper fiction was published after the acquittal of Borden. In this version of the story, unlike "Ruth Herrick's Assignment," no deep sense of sympathy flowers between the reporter and the female suspect, and the accused criminal does not offer a suppressed confession. Rather, the interview leads Iverson to grow even more convinced of Mrs. Brandow's innocence. Later, her editor remarks, "What a problem it would have put up to you if she *had* been guilty and *had* confessed! On the one hand, loyalty to the *Searchlight*—you'd have had to publish the news. On the other hand, sympathy for the woman—for it would be you who sent her to the electric chair, or remained silent and saved her."[45] Here is precisely the quandary Jordan poses in "Ruth Herrick's Assignment," where Herrick must decide which value will transcend the other, loyalty to the paper or justifiable sympathy toward the injured woman—and, by extension, commitment to a superior kind of journalism as well. Moreover, in this telling of the tale, the editor introduces his anxieties about women in the newsroom—nothing, in his mind, can guarantee that a woman is finally capable of producing hard news.

A coworker encourages Iverson to turn the tale of her encounter with Mrs. Brandow into a magazine story and to speculate in fiction about what would have happened if the woman *had* confessed to murder. Once again, Jordan teases the reader with narrative layers, since in real life Jordan did indeed write a magazine tale about an encounter with an accused woman. Iverson submits her story—presumably the same plot as in "Ruth Herrick's Assignment"—to a periodical that holds it for a year until after the acquittal of Mrs. Brandow. And when Iverson's fictional tale emerges in print, a great outcry erupts in the newsroom, as it did for Jordan when "Ruth Herrick's Assignment" appeared after Borden's acquittal. Iverson's editor is incensed, believing she has "throw[n] us down on this story," that she placed personal loyalty to a sympathetic female figure above loyalty to the newspaper.[46]

Iverson convinces her editor that no such thing has happened, that the story was a fiction. But her troubles are only beginning. Other reporters have also read the piece, and they insist that "the story read like the real thing!" In a final twist, Iverson goes to see Mrs. Brandow, worried the story has been widely misinterpreted by the general public, as well, and has caused significant discomfort for Mrs. Brandow in her post-acquittal life. The journalist somewhat disingenuously apologizes to Mrs. Brandow, saying, "It never occurred to me that any one would connect a fiction story with—with your case." But something else has never occurred to Iverson: the possibility that perhaps, in her fiction, she was right all along about Mrs. Brandow's guilt. As Mrs. Brandow leaves her meeting with Iverson, she leans in and whispers, "Oh, wise young judge! . . . Tell me, before we part—how did you know?"[47] Mrs. Brandow is guilty after all. May Iverson's story, fictionalized as it is, still hit the truth.

Besides serving as the final chapter in the intertwined stories of Elizabeth Jordan, Lizzie Borden, women's journalistic sympathy, and newspaper fiction, the tale of May Iverson and Helen Brandow was the result of an understandable impulse on Jordan's part to return to her earlier tale. In the aftermath of the Borden trial, readers naturally drew a direct link between the story and Jordan's coverage of an actual murder case, a link not supported by the compositional timeline, since publishers, again, delayed the release of Jordan's Ruth Herrick story until after the trial. Some readers—and many of Jordan's male colleagues—grew convinced that weak, womanly sympathy had undermined her abilities as a journalist. No evidence suggests Jordan ever believed, despite the plot lines of her short stories, that Lizzie Borden was in fact guilty and had duped the reporter.

Readers were correct, of course, in noting the similar narrative frameworks that appear in both Jordan's newspaper fictions and her newspaper articles. Those connections are far from coincidental. If "Ruth Herrick's Assignment" was not inspired by Jordan's coverage of the Borden trial, her news dispatches from the trial certainly *do* seem influenced by the newspaper fiction she had penned. In an intricate blending of fact, fiction, reportage, and storytelling, Jordan constructed an elaborate meta-narrative about sensationalism, news "objectivity," women's reporting, and the role of sympathy in reading the accused criminal both fictionally and factually. June Howard remarks that Jordan repeatedly tested "distinctions like public and private," ultimately "remapping spheres to make room for the professional woman."[48] But she also strove to refine private newspaper reading, in order to influence and reform public response. By coincidentally linking sympathy with the relentless pursuit of factuality, Jordan sought a critical reading and dismantled lingering ideas about the nature of female professionalism within a literary marketplace that increasingly prized "the real thing" or "True Stories of the News," in fiction and journalism alike. In her final analysis, Jordan argued for sympathy as a critical component of reporting—and, coincidentally, justified a desk of her own in the late nineteenth-century newsroom.

Afterword

Stories came so thick and fast they grew very unimportant.
People's life secrets and their heartaches and their emotions were shuffled and juggled
around and then scrapped in such a hurry that one lost all personal reaction to them.

—Mildred Gilman, *Sob Sister*

In her 1931 novel *Sob Sister,* American author Mildred Gilman pictures the life of hard-nosed female reporter Jane Ray as she struggles to balance career ambitions and personal emotions. Essentially married to her job writing for one of New York's leading papers, Ray has grown tired of the endless stream of stories that finally offer little significance. Emotion has, for the newspaper woman, become a commodity, something to be "shuffled" and "juggled" and ultimately "scrapped" as the public voraciously consumes sensational news, "eat[ing]" it "with its morning toast and drink[ing] it with its breakfast coffee." Ray is a sob sister, a female reporter whose job depends on the excessive display of emotion. However, Ray's attempts at professional sympathy lack genuine, lasting feeling. She has perfected instead the kind of calculated sympathy that Bly's work sometimes features, rather than the deeper identification offered in Fuller's, Fern's, and Jordan's best reporting. In her visit to a jail, for instance, Ray notes, "the cells were too small and stifling and dark. There was no running water. . . . Jane Ray thought she was sincere when she sympathized [with the prisoner] about how awful it was. In reality, she was much more excited by the story. The heat and stench and the iron bars made good adjectives for the story."[1] Where some other female journalists would turn the spectacle of the suffering prisoner into an occasion for fellow feeling and a call for reform,

Ray's sympathy is a commodity churned out for readers in as dramatic a fashion as possible, something she finally cannot even recognize as real (or not) within herself. The newspaper industry has reduced human suffering to snappy adjectives and good copy.

The title of Gilman's novel and her protagonist's attitude toward scenes of human suffering point toward a feminized newspaper cliché that grew almost directly out of one of the reportorial styles Nellie Bly initiated: the sob sister. Coined in 1907 to describe the emotionally fraught articles published by Annie Laurie (Winifred Black Bonfils), Dorothea Dix, Ada Paterson, Nixola Greeley-Smith (the granddaughter of Horace Greeley), and other women, critics used the phrase "sob sister" pejoratively, to describe *apparently* sympathetic writing, vivid emotion expressed in the name of selling papers. The most famous display of sob sister reporting occurred during the trial of Harry Thaw, accused of murdering the architect Stanford White in response to a dalliance between Thaw and White's wife, Evelyn. In the words of Ishbel Ross, the newspaper women who covered the case "spread their sympathy like jam."[2] The "hard-boiled sob sister" was a reporter "who could stare at all manner of corpses without wincing, one who could calmly write her notes, fighting for names and addresses while rescuers disentangled victims from wrecks," and "pour more anguish into the copy" and "more emotional feeling" than any man could—or at least the semblance of such.[3] It was through apparent, but ultimately superficial, emotional response to jarring, sensationalistic news that sob sisters defended space for themselves as newspaper women in the early twentieth-century newsroom. In some sense, it was a writing style that had evolved, for better or for worse, out of the more complex sympathy that Fuller, Fern, Bly, and Jordan had each expressed as part of their own professional repertoires.

The label "sob sister," as Patricia Bradley contends, "served to define female reporters" and to imply that women could only "write in emotional terms because that was what their nature demanded."[4] Here was the same argument lobbed against female reporters throughout the nineteenth century, but where such authors as Fuller, Fern, Bly, and Jordan redirected "female nature" for their own ends, to gain entry and authority in a male-dominated profession, the sob sisters' use of sympathy was not, in the long run, as professionally productive. As much as they loved the maudlin reports filed by these newspaper women, critical readers recognized that the emotion behind the words was disingenuous. Lacking the valuable advice about the use of emotion that Jordan had received as a novice reporter—let the readers shed their own tears—sob sisters merged sentimentality with journalism to an astonishing extreme. They were paid for emotional connections with the subjects of news stories; that emotion was, in fact, explicitly commodified. In effect, the sob sisters expressed a sympathy predicated on sensation and celebrity, rather than the more self-reflective alliance between an article's writer, subject, and audience. As a character in Gilman's novel protests, "The sympathy you feel for human beings is paid sympathy. It looks real to them. They don't know it's all part of earning your salary. They fall for it and give you the story."[5]

Even as women like Jordan and Bly built on the strategies Fuller and Fern had constructed, the rise of an increasingly commercialized and sensational press at the turn of the century marginalized some women in the mainstream press even further. The overwrought emotionality of sob sister reporting clashed with shifting journalistic standards and an emerging commitment to "objectivity" that papers simultaneously reinforced and masculinized in the early years of the twentieth century. A new institutional discourse emerged, one "that privileged a detached reporting style which was out of sync with the modus operandi of the sensational journals most likely to hire female reporters," as Jean Marie Lutes astutely describes.[6] Female reporters, particularly those who continued to engage readers with a sympathetic tone, became easy targets for audiences eager to identify women with emotion and to insist, as well, that women were incapable of meeting the increasingly stringent demands of twentieth-century journalistic professionalism.

Nevertheless, as the era of the sob sister ended—at least officially—in the first quarter of the twentieth century, the number of female reporters working for mainstream newspapers rose. By the second decade of the new century, New York became "a veritable showcase for first-rate women reporters." Readers and managing editors gradually abandoned the idea of feminine sympathy in the newsroom, and "by the 1920s and 1930s the idea that women must write differently from men had been overcome."[7] Working within an environment that increasingly rewarded the detached voice of the writer sympathy—and that eventually understood women could meet these standards just as well as men—no longer seemed relevant as a discursive professional strategy. Women, in some sense, lost the need for sympathy as a subversive tool in the face of modern press standardization.

Still, in comparing women's sympathetic writing at different points in the nineteenth century, historians of journalism and literature should recognize the power that Fuller, Fern, Bly, and Jordan tapped into as they sought to lend their voices to the news. Their calculated deployment of sympathy helped them position themselves as gendered subjects within the profession. At the same time, in writing for the newspapers and in commenting upon public issues, they became part of that public, despite—indeed, *because* of—the use of language that had been tied, ideologically, to frail femininity. The four journalists I study here yield case studies not only in making the newspaper women's business, but also in how, even in the use of that tradition, they exposed and transgressed the porous boundaries between female and male, private and public, newsroom and asylum cell, parlor and prison.

Notes

1. "Discomfiture of an Editress," *Frank Leslie's Illustrated Newspaper,* Sept. 3, 1859.

2. Jeffrey L. Pasley, *"The Tyranny of Printers": Newspaper Politics in the Early American Republic* (Charlottesville: Univ. of Virginia Press, 2001), 7. Andrew R. L. Cayton adds that in reality women "were active participants in the political debates of the 1790s; they marched in parades, read newspapers, wrote pamphlets" ("We Are All Nationalists, We Are All Localists," review of David Waldstreicher, *In the Midst of Perpetual Fetes: The Making of American Nationalism, 1776–1820, Journal of the Early Republic* 18, no. 3 (1998): 524.

3. Despite the importance of women as not only readers but reporters, surprisingly few full-length works have been written about their historical role in newspaper journalism, especially of the eighteenth and nineteenth centuries. Some studies of note include Alice Fahs, *Out on Assignment: Newspaper Women and the Making of Modern Public Space* (Chapel Hill: Univ. of North Carolina Press, 2011); Jan Whitt, *Women in American Journalism: A New History* (Urbana: Univ. of Illinois Press, 2008); Jean Marie Lutes, *Front-Page Girls: Women Journalists in American Culture and Fiction, 1880–1930* (Ithaca, NY: Cornell Univ. Press, 2006); Patricia Bradley, *Women and the Press: The Struggle for Equality* (Evanston, IL: Northwestern Univ. Press, 2005); Maurine H. Beasley and Shelia J. Gibbons, *Taking Their Place: A Documentary History of Women and Journalism* (Washington, DC: American Univ. Press, 1993); Kay Mills, *A Place in the News: From the*

Women's Pages to the Front Page (New York: Dodd, Mead, 1988); and Marion Marzolf, *Up from the Footnote: A History of Women Journalists* (New York: Hastings House, 1977).

4. Qtd. in Marzolf, *Up from the Footnote*, 1.

5. David Paul Nord, *Communities of Journalism: A History of American Newspapers and Their Readers* (Urbana: Univ. of Illinois Press, 2001), 88.

6. Isabelle Lehuu, *Carnival on the Page: Popular Print Media in Antebellum America* (Chapel Hill: Univ. of North Carolina Press, 2000), 16. In contrast, London printed only sixty-three thousand dailies for its population of 2.3 million.

7. Paula Kopacz, "Feminist at the *Tribune*: Margaret Fuller as Professional Writer," *Studies in the American Renaissance* 20 (1991): 123.

8. Beasley and Gibbons, *Taking Their Place*, 8.

9. See Elizabeth V. Burt, *Women's Press Organizations, 1881–1999* (Westport, CT: Greenwood, 2000), xviii. Women also continued to have an important presence in rural areas, a subject ripe for research. See, for instance, Madelon Golden Schlipp and Sharon M. Murphy, *Great Women of the Press* (Carbondale: Southern Illinois Univ. Press, 1983), xi.

10. Lehuu, *Carnival on the Page*, 30.

11. Fahs, *Out on Assignment*, 17; Elizabeth Jordan, "The Newspaper Woman's Story," *Lippincott's Monthly Magazine* 51 (Mar. 1893): 340.

12. Jordan, "Newspaper Woman's Story," 340.

13. Bradley, *Women and the Press*, 132.

14. Qtd. in Deborah Chambers, Linda Steiner, and Carole Fleming, *Women and Journalism* (London: Routledge, 2004), 14, 16.

15. Margaret W. Welch, "Is Newspaper Work Healthful for Women?" *Journal of Social Science* 32 (Nov. 1894): 110.

16. George Gordon-Smith, "Psychological Sentimentalism: Consciousness, Affect, and the Sentimental Henry James," in *Sentimentalism in Nineteenth-Century America: Literary and Cultural Practices*, ed. Mary G. De Jong and Paula Bernat Bennett (Madison, NJ: Fairleigh Dickinson Univ. Press, 2013), 183.

17. David Marshall, *The Surprising Effects of Sympathy: Marivaux, Diderot, Rousseau, and Mary Shelley* (Chicago: Univ. of Chicago Press, 1988), 3.

18. Julia Stern, *The Plight of Feeling: Sympathy and Dissent in the Early American Novel* (Chicago: Univ. of Chicago Press, 1997), 7.

19. Glenn Hendler, *Public Sentiments: Structures of Feeling in Nineteenth-Century American Literature* (Chapel Hill: Univ. of North Carolina Press, 2001), 128.

20. Joanne Dobson, "Reclaiming Sentimental Literature," *American Literature* 69, no. 2 (1997): 283; Mary G. De Jong, introduction to *Sentimentalism in Nineteenth-Century America: Literary and Cultural Practices*, ed. Mary G. De Jong and Paula Bernat Bennett (Madison, NJ: Fairleigh Dickinson Univ. Press, 2013), 2; Shirley Samuels, *The Culture of Sentiment: Race, Gender, and Sentimentality in Nineteenth-Century America* (New York: Oxford University Press, 1992), 4.

21. June Howard, "What Is Sentimentality," *American Literary History* 11, no. 1 (1999): 73.

22. Hendler, *Public Sentiments,* 20. See also Elizabeth Barnes, *States of Sympathy: Seduction and Democracy in the American Novel* (New York: Columbia Univ. Press, 1997), and Mary Chapman and Glenn Hendler, eds. *Sentimental Men: Masculinity and the Politics of Affect in American Culture* (Berkeley: Univ. of California Press, 1999).

23. Fahs, *Out on Assignment,* 12.

24. Barbara Welter, *Dimity Convictions: The American Woman in the Nineteenth Century* (Athens: Ohio Univ. Press, 1976); Nancy F. Cott, *The Bonds of Womanhood: Woman's Sphere in New England, 1780–1825* (New Haven: Yale Univ. Press, 1977); Mary P. Ryan, *The Empire of the Mother: American Writing about Domesticity, 1830–1860* (New York: Harrington Park Press, 1985); Jane Tompkins, *Sensational Designs: The Cultural Work of American Fiction, 1790–1860* (New York: Oxford Univ. Press, 1986). For challenges to the paradigms of earlier critics, see, for instance, Monika M. Elbert, ed., *Separate Spheres No More: Gender Convergence in American Literature, 1830–1930* (Tuscaloosa: Univ. of Alabama Press, 2000). Faye Halpern, however, contends in *Sentimental Readers: The Rise, Fall, and Revival of a Disparaged Rhetoric* (Iowa City: Univ. of Iowa Press, 2013) that "we might still gingerly use the term 'true womanhood,'" understanding that it was less "a lived reality" than "an ideal accessible to some women and not to others. . . . [W]hile sentimental rhetoric is not inextricably tied to the domestic, pious, pure, and 'submissive' woman—she does allow it to flourish" (67).

25. Linda Kerber, "Separate Spheres, Female Worlds, Women's Place: The Rhetoric of Women's History," *Journal of American History* 75, no. 1 (1988): 17, 18.

26. Suzanne Keen, *Empathy and the Novel* (New York: Oxford Univ. Press, 2007), xi.

27. Elizabeth Barnes, *States of Sympathy: Seduction and Democracy in the American Novel* (New York: Columbia Univ. Press, 1997), 4. Whether or not sympathy-producing scenes could create actual change is open to debate.

28. De Jong, introduction, 3.

29. Keen, *Empathy and the Novel,* 47.

30. De Jong, introduction, 3.

31. See Meredith McGill, *American Literature and the Culture of Reprinting, 1834–1853* (Philadelphia: Univ. of Pennsylvania Press, 2002), for a splendid discussion of republishing in the antebellum period. Lacking firmly established national and international copyright laws, the "culture of reprinting" continued throughout most of the century.

32. Nerone and Barnhurst add that as the century progressed, "the categories of correspondent and reporter began to blur" as "reporters acquired some of the privilege and prestige of the correspondent, along with something of an authorial voice," until "the designation 'correspondent' came to refer to newsgathering in

addition to letter writing and commentary" John Nerone and Kevin G. Barnhurst, "US Newspaper Types, the Newsroom, and the Division of Labor, 1750–2000," *Journalism Studies* 4, no. 4 (2003): 444.

33. June Howard, *Publishing the Family* (Durham, NC: Duke Univ. Press, 2001), 2.

1. Representing Institutions

1. In the early and mid-nineteenth century, doctors "differentiated the three main forms of insanity" by the terms "mania, melancholia, and dementia" (Lynn Gamwell and Nancy Tomes, *Madness in America: Cultural and Medical Perceptions of Mental Illness before 1914* [Ithaca, NY: Cornell Univ. Press, 1995], 71). While melancholics tended to receive the most sympathy from members of the general public, "maniacs"—what we might now suppose to be people in psychotic or possibly manic states, generally prompted representation filled with terror or repulsion. By the nineteenth century, Americans commonly used the words "insanity," "lunacy," and "madness" to "describe what we today call mental illness," though these words sometimes "had a different connotation" depending on context and the expertise of the person using them. During the first half of the nineteenth century, the doctors who headed asylums were called "asylum superintendents," and the term "psychiatrist," which was first used in German academic circles mid-century, eventually traveled to American medical circles later in the century (ibid., 9).

2. Debra Bernardi and Jill Bergman, "Introduction: Benevolence Literature by American Women," in *Our Sisters' Keepers: Nineteenth-Century Benevolence Literature by American Women*, ed. Jill Bergman and Debra Bernardi (Tuscaloosa: Univ. of Alabama Press, 2005), 8. The reality of the "private sphere" / "public sphere" split is, of course, complicated since, as Linda Kerber, explains, "women's allegedly 'separate sphere' was affected by what men did, and how activities defined by women in their own sphere influenced and even set constraints and limitations on what men might choose to do" (Linda K. Kerber, "Separate Spheres, Female Worlds, Woman's Place: The Rhetoric of Women's History," *Journal of American History* 75, no. 1 (1988): 17, 18).

3. Rosemarie Garland Thomson, "Crippled Girls and Lame Old Women: Sentimental Spectacles of Sympathy in Nineteenth-Century American Women's Writing," in *Nineteenth-Century American Women Writers: A Critical Reader*, ed. Karen L. Kilkup (Maiden, MA: Blackwell, 1998), 128, 131.

4. Benjamin Reiss, *Theaters of Madness: Insane Asylums and Nineteenth-Century American Culture* (Chicago: Univ. of Chicago Press, 2007), 178. For further discussion of women's involvement in prison reform, see Estelle B. Freedman, *Their Sisters' Keepers: Women's Prison Reform in America, 1830–1930* (Ann Arbor: Univ. of Michigan Press, 1984).

5. Wendy Mitchinson, "Gender and Insanity as Characteristics of the Insane: A Nineteenth-Century Case," *Canadian Bulletin of Medical History* 4, no. 2 (1987): 101.

6. Reiss, *Theaters of Madness,* 178.

7. Oliver Sacks, introduction to *Asylum: Inside the Closed World of State Mental Hospitals* (Cambridge: Massachusetts Institute of Technology Press, 2009). I wish to acknowledge the centrality of Foucault's writing about asylums, prisons, and social control in discussions of these institutions; however my discussion of asylums and prisons sets aside Foucault's institutional histories in favor of direct investigation of how periodical writers represented institutional life. As historians like Wendy Mitchinson have already noted, despite the intriguing nature of Foucault's theories of incarceration and control, in historical reality, the nineteenth-century American "asylum was not . . . used as a place to hide away the deviant or the idle . . . except to the extent that mental illness was defined as deviancy and led to an inability to work" ("Gender and Insanity as Characteristics of the Insane," 99). Likewise, Caleb Smith asserts that scholars must problematize Foucault's theories—in this case, about the prison—"as a subject-making institution." See Caleb Smith, *The Prison and the American Imagination* (New Haven: Yale Univ. Press, 2009), 4. Janet Floyd adds that "the contemporary response" to public institutions "was much more diverse, much more attentive to its specificities, than the response of scholars of our own day," including Foucault, would suggest (Janet Floyd, "Dislocations of the Self: Eliza Farnham at Sing Sing Prison," *Journal of American Studies* 40, no. 2 [2006]: 311–25). Edward Shorter, likewise, dismisses "the social constructionists who claim that psychiatry's apparent good intentions were a sham, a pretense for gaining professional power" (Shorter, *A History of Psychiatry: From the Era of the Asylum to the Age of Prozac* [Hoboken, NJ: Wiley, 1988], 34).

8. Shorter, *History of Psychiatry,* 46.

9. Gamwell and Tomes, *Madness in America,* 37. It is worth noting that in nineteenth-century America, as now, "large numbers of the insane were held in prisons," so discussion of asylum reform often went hand in hand with discussion of prison reform. See Reiss, *Theaters of Madness,* 1.

10. Samantha Boardman and George J. Makari, "The Lunatic Asylum on Blackwell's Island and the New York Press," *American Journal of Psychiatry* 164, no. 4 (2007): 581. Further discussion of "moral treatment" is available in Reiss, *Theaters of Madness,* 4–5, and Shorter, *A History of Psychiatry,* 18–22 and 43–46. An 1874 article written "By a Lunatic" describes "Insanity: Its Moral Treatment" from the point of view of a patient (*Phrenological Journal and Science of Health* [Jan. 1874]: 40–45).

11. W. H. Davenport, "Blackwell's Island Lunatic Asylum," *Harper's New Monthly Magazine,* Feb. 1866, 277.

12. David J. Rothman, *The Discovery of the Asylum: Social Order and Disorder in the New Republic* (Boston: Little, Brown, 1990), 239.

13. Gamwell and Tomes, *Madness in America,* 9.

14. "An Insane Convict's Bloody Work," *New York Times,* Dec. 15, 1884; "Maniac Runs Amuck," *New York Times,* June 25, 1900; "A Maniac's Deeds of Blood," *Chicago Daily Tribune,* June 20, 1887; "Strangled by a Maniac," *New York Times,* Oct. 11, 1897.

15. Reiss, *Theaters of Madness,* 13.

16. Gamwell and Tomes, *Madness in America,* 35. In France, arguably the most famous example of asylum tourism lies in Jean-Martin Charcot's "hysterics" on display in the late nineteenth century at Paris's Pitié-Salpêtrière Hospital.

17. Qtd. in Reiss, *Theaters of Madness,* 13.

18. Davenport, "Blackwell's Island Lunatic Asylum," 278–79.

19. See, for instance, James Miller, *Miller's New York As It Is* (New York: James Miller, 1880), 46–47, and *The Englishman's Illustrated Guide Book to the United States and Canada* (London: Longmans, Green, Reader & Dyer, 1880). Janet Miron offers a fascinating study of asylum tourism in *Prisons, Asylums, and the Public: Institutional Visiting in the Nineteenth Century* (Toronto: Univ. of Toronto Press, 2011).

20. Reiss, *Theaters of Madness,* 13. The families of patients, however, "were generally not allowed to visit, as the superintendents feared that they would create obstacles to treatment" (13).

21. Davenport, "Blackwell's Island Lunatic Asylum," 294.

22. Virginia De Forrest, "Visit to a Lunatic Asylum—A True Sketch," *Lady's Home Magazine,* Feb. 1858, 103.

23. "A Visit to the Lunatic Asylum on Blackwell's Island," *Harper's Weekly,* Mar. 19, 1859, 184.

24. "How to See New York," *Scribner's Monthly,* June 1876, 273–74.

25. Irenaeus, "The Insane on Blackwell's Island," *New York Observer and Chronicle,* Mar. 29, 1845.

26. Irenaeus, "An Hour in an Insane Asylum," *New York Observer and Chronicle,* May 24, 1845.

27. Boardman and Makari, "Lunatic Asylum on Blackwell's Island," 50.

28. Davenport, "Blackwell's Island Lunatic Asylum," 283. "Mrs. Buchanan" makes an appearance in the March 19, 1859, *Harper's Weekly* article as well, with the reminder that "most people have heard of Mrs. Buchanan" (186).

29. Charles W. Coyle, "Life in an Insane Asylum," *Overland Monthly and Out West Magazine* 21 (Feb. 1893): 165.

30. Davenport, "Blackwell's Island Lunatic Asylum," 280, 279.

31. Ibid., 279.

32. "Visit to the Lunatic Asylum on Blackwell's Island," 186.

33. Davenport, "Blackwell's Island Lunatic Asylum," 288.

34. Ibid., 186; Edward M. Franklin, "The Madhouse, and Its Inmates," *Ballou's Dollar Monthly Magazine* 15, no. 1 (Jan. 1862): 79.

35. See, for instance, an 1842 article that directs its readers, "Come with me, gentle reader, beneath this clump of trees, and we will survey the prisoners as they come forth," an activity that, the author insists, must occur with the purest forms of sympathy ("Blackwell's Island," *American Magazine and Repository of Useful Literature*, Apr. 1842, 67). "Hours in a Mad-House," *Christian Parlor Magazine*, Apr. 1846, describes the moral treatment instituted by Pliny Earle at the Bloomingdale Asylum and exclaims that "the heartstrings are torn with sympathy" at the sight of the hospital's inmates (368). Even the writer of this article, however, sees a dance at the asylum as "the highest degree amusing to contemplate" and prizes "preaching to the insane" above all others (369).

36. Coyle, "Life in an Insane Asylum," 161.

37. Franklin, "Madhouse, and Its Inmates," 79.

38. Karen Tracey, "Stories of the Poorhouse," in Bergman and Bernardi, *Our Sisters' Keepers*, 23.

39. Floyd, "Dislocations of the Self," 320.

40. Coyle, "Life in an Insane Asylum," 168.

41. "Hours in a Mad-House."

42. Alice Maud Meadows, "The Romance of a Mad-House," *Once a Week*, Feb. 2, 1892, 15.

43. Bella Rose Florence, "The Maniac's Confession," *Peterson's Magazine*, May 1858, 364, 366.

44. T. Hood, "A Tale of Terror," *Albion*, Dec. 25, 1841, 455.

45. "A Fellow-Passenger," *Youth's Companion*, May 29, 1879: 178–79.

46. Scott Way, "A Madman's Story," *Puck*, Sept. 8, 1886: 21; "A Keeper's Story," *Massachusetts Ploughman and New England Journal of Agriculture*, Mar. 25, 1871, 4; "A Night with a Maniac," *Knickerbocker; or, New York Monthly Magazine* 5, no. 3 (Mar. 1835): 221–30; "An Encounter with a Madman," *Cincinnati Weekly Herald and Philanthropist*, Dec. 18, 1844, 1.

47. Davenport, "Blackwell's Island Lunatic Asylum," 294.

48. Reiss, *Theaters of Madness*, 169, 180, 184. Scores of newspaper and journal articles and memoirs also exposed and denounced the practice of false commitments to asylums.

49. In addition to an unknown number of short stories and fictional sketches published in periodicals, some of the many nineteenth-century novels about insanity and asylums include Amelia Bristow, *The Maniac, a Tale* (1810); *Mary the Maniac* (1843); *Julia, the Maniac* (1847); Amelia Alderson Opie, *The Gentleman's Daughter, or, A City's Great Temptations* (1845); Alexander Ross, *Recollections of an Ex-Maniac, and Other Tales* (1858); Mary Elizabeth Braddon, *Lady Audley's Secret* (1862); Charles Reade, *Very Hard Cash* (1863); William Gilbert, *The Monomaniac: or, Shirley Hall Asylum* (1864); Margaret Blount, *The Maniac Bride, or, The Dead Secret of Hollow Ash Hall* (1870); Martha E. Berry, *Bella, or, The Cradle of Liberty, a Story of Insane Asylums* (1874); Clara Burnham, *A Sane Lunatic* (1882);

A Palace-Prison (1884); *Wed to a Lunatic: A Wild, Weird Yarn of Love* (1896); J. Storer Clouston, *The Lunatic at Large: A Novel* (1899); Headon Hill, *Caged! The Romance of a Lunatic Asylum* (1900).

50. "What Is Really Bad in Fiction," *American Builder and Journal of Art,* Apr. 1, 1873.

51. "Madness in Novels," *Littell's Living Age,* Apr. 21, 1866, 180.

52. Floyd, "Dislocations of the Self," 313.

53. Jennifer Rae Greeson, "The 'Mysteries and Miseries' of North Carolina: New York City, Urban Gothic Fiction, and *Incidents in the Life of a Slave Girl,*" *American Literature* 73 (June 2001): 280–81. One of the best studies of the urban gothic novel is in David Reynolds's *Beneath the American Renaissance: The Subversive Imagination in the Age of Emerson and Melville* (New York: Knopf, 1988). It would be a mistake to believe, of course, that the mass media were the only periodicals that cast aspersions on criminals, as exemplified by a quote from the *Christian Union:* "The thought crosses one's mind, in the midst of the unnatural quiet" of a chapel service, "What a slumbering volcano of depravity is here! And what a horrible eruption of profanity and hate and uncleanness and deviltry of all kinds would it emit if all restraint were removed!" (H. H. Moore, "Sunday on 'The Island,'" *Christian Union,* Oct. 11, 1883, 286).

54. Joseph Valente, "The Novel and the Police (Gazette)," *Novel* 29, no. 1 (1995): 13.

55. W. David Lewis, *From Newgate to Dannemora: The Rise of the Penitentiary in New York, 1796–1848* (Ithaca, NY: Cornell Univ. Press, 1965), 158, 159.

56. Articles about prostitution, particularly at the beginning of the century, typically used coded language in making reference to this particular crime, using words like "social evil," "moral insanity," "unfortunates," and "Magdalenes."

57. "Visit to the Lunatic Asylum on Blackwell's Island," 185.

58. Karen J. Renner, "Seduction, Prostitution, and the Control of Female Desire in Popular Antebellum Fiction," *Nineteenth-Century Literature* 65, no. 2 (2010): 166, 168, 170.

59. "A Sabbath Scene on Blackwell's Island," *Ladies' Repository,* Dec. 1853, 552.

60. The article's author does not extend the same courtesy to the male inmates who are attending the chapel service, whom she characterizes as "sullen."

61. "The Tombs," *Prisoner's Friend,* Oct. 1, 1849, 73, 75, 77.

62. Many other articles used direct addresses to readers, inviting them to enter the prison with the article writer. See, for example, "Blackwell's Island," 67–69.

63. Lydia Maria Child, *Letters from New-York* (London: Richard Bentley, 1843), 212. For a fuller discussion of Child's rhetorical stance, see Heather Roberts, "'The Public Heart': Urban Life and the Politics of Sympathy in Lydia Maria Child's *Letters from New York,*" *American Literature* 76 (Dec. 2004): 749–75.

64. Child, *Letters from New-York,* 213, 212. Patricia Cline Cohen, Timothy Gilfoyle, and Helen Lefkowitz Horowitz offer a lively study of these "sporty" newspapers in *The Flash Press: Sporting Male Weeklies in 1840s New York* (Chicago: Univ. of Chicago Press, 2008).

2. Scenes of Sympathy

1. Margaret Fuller, *Woman in the Nineteenth Century,* in *The Essential Margaret Fuller,* ed. Jeffrey Steele (New Brunswick, NJ: Rutgers Univ. Press, 1992), 296, 307.

2. Fuller continued her connection with the *New-York Tribune* until 1850, but not as a salaried employee. After leaving for Europe in 1846, she sent occasional letters detailing political conditions in Italy. By 1844 America had seen a number of women who had authored travel letters or occasional essays, but Fuller was the first woman to write regularly for a paper on a formal, professional basis. The official name and spelling of the paper in which she wrote was the *New-York Daily Tribune,* as opposed to the *Weekly Tribune,* a national paper. I will refer to this paper as the *New-York Tribune,* by which I mean the daily, urban edition.

3. The significant exception to this rule would be alternative and reformist papers, such as Lydia Maria Child's *National Anti-Slavery Standard.*

4. Judith Mattson Bean and Joel Myerson call Fuller's work on the *Tribune* a "redefinition of political discourse as women's work." See Bean and Myerson, introduction to *Margaret Fuller, Critic: Writings from the* New-York Tribune, *1844–1846,* ed. Judith Mattson Bean and Joel Myerson (New York: Columbia Univ. Press, 2000), xx.

5. Although some articles in the *Tribune* were identified by the author's initials, full bylines would not come into vogue until the late nineteenth century, when reporters started to gain celebrity status in such papers as Joseph Pulitzer's *New York World* and William Randolph Hearst's *New York Journal.*

6. Qtd. in Charles Capper, *Margaret Fuller, an American Romantic Life: The Public Years* (New York: Oxford Univ. Press, 2007), 198.

7. Qtd. in Bell Gale Chevigny, *The Woman and the Myth: Margaret Fuller's Life and Writings,* rev. ed. (Boston: Northeastern Univ. Press, 1994), 307; Margaret Fuller, "Darkness Visible," *New-York Tribune,* Mar. 10, 1846.

8. Fuller, *Woman in the Nineteenth Century,* 320.

9. Robert J. Scholnick, "'The Ultraism of the Day': Greene's *Boston Post,* Hawthorne, Fuller, Melville, Stowe, and Literary Journalism in Antebellum America," *American Periodicals* 18, no. 2 (2008): 189.

10. Margaret Fuller, 1845 letter, in *The Letters of Margaret Fuller,* ed. Robert H. Hudspeth, vol. 4 of 6, *1845–1847* (Ithaca, NY: Cornell Univ. Press, 1987), 39–40. Fuller's reach actually extended far beyond the city, since Greeley reprinted her articles in the *Weekly Tribune,* a vastly popular national paper. See Capper, *Margaret Fuller, an American Romantic Life,* 198.

11. Qtd. in Barbara Belford, *Brilliant Bylines: A Biographical Anthology of Notable Newspaper-Women in America* (New York: Columbia Univ. Press, 1986), 11. The definitive biography of Fuller is Charles Capper's masterful two-volume work, but other valuable sources include Paula Blanchard's *Margaret Fuller: From Transcendentalism*

to Revolution (New York: Delacorte, 1978), and Joan von Mehren's *Minerva and the Muse: A Life of Margaret Fuller* (Amherst: Univ. of Massachusetts Press, 1994).

12. Steven Fink, "Margaret Fuller: The Evolution of a Woman of Letters," in *Reciprocal Influences: Literary Production, Distribution, and Consumption in America,* ed. Steven Fink and Susan S. Williams (Columbus: Ohio State Univ. Press, 1999), 60; Susan S. Williams, *Reclaiming Authorship: Literary Women in America, 1850–1900* (Philadelphia: Univ. of Pennsylvania Press, 2006), 44. Joan von Mehren provides a pithy description of the Conversations in *Minerva and the Muse,* 114–15.

13. Horace Greeley, *Recollections of a Busy Life* (New York: J. B. Ford, 1868), 169.

14. Larry J. Reynolds, "From *Dial* Essay to New York Book: The Making of *Woman in the Nineteenth Century,*" in *Periodical Literature in Nineteenth-Century America,* ed. Kenneth M. Price and Susan Belasco Smith (Charlottesville: Univ. Press of Virginia, 1995), 17. For information on Fuller's work with the *Dial* and revisions to "The Great Lawsuit," see Sylvia Jenkins Cook, *Working Women, Literary Ladies: The Industrial Revolution and Female Aspiration* (New York: Oxford Univ. Press, 2008); Joel Myerson, *The New England Transcendentalists and the* Dial*: A History of the Magazine and Its Contributors.* Madison, NJ: Fairleigh Dickinson Press, 1980; and Capper, *Margaret Fuller, An American Romantic Life,* 3–6.

15. Greeley, *Recollections of a Busy Life,* 175.

16. Qtd. in Cook, *Working Women, Literary Ladies,* 95; von Mehren, *Minerva and the Muse,* 194.

17. Barbara Packer, *The Transcendentalists* (Athens: Univ. of Georgia Press, 2007), 130.

18. See, for instance, Capper, *Margaret Fuller, An American Romantic,* 194–213, and Susan Belasco, "'The Animating Influences of Discord': Margaret Fuller in 1844," *Legacy* 20, nos. 1 & 2 (2003): 85, 87. Belasco points to 1844 as a critical year in Fuller's shift from private to public, while Capper examines 1840 as the initiation of a remarkable transition point.

19. Qtd. in Capper, *Margaret Fuller, An American Romantic,* 3.

20. Jeffrey Steele, *Transfiguring America: Myth, Ideology, and Mourning in Margaret Fuller's Writing* (Columbia: Univ. of Missouri Press, 2001), 234. Benjamin Reiss remarks that one reason many transcendentalists were interested in asylum reform, in particular, was that "key members" of the movement "faced the specter of institutionalization in asylums for their loved ones, followers, and even themselves" (*Theaters of Madness: Insane Asylums and Nineteenth-Century American Culture* [Chicago: Univ. of Chicago Press, 2007], 103).

21. Catherine C. Mitchell, *Margaret Fuller's New York Journalism: A Biographical Essay and Key Writings* (Knoxville: Univ. of Tennessee Press, 1995), 12.

22. Michael Schudson, *Discovering the News: A Social History of American Newspapers* (New York: Basic Books, 1978), 18. For information about the moon hoax, see Matthew Goodman's *The Sun and the Moon: The Remarkable True Account of*

Hoaxers, Showmen, Dueling Journalists, and Lunar Man-Bats in Nineteenth-Century New York (New York: Basic Books, 2008).

23. Amy Gilman Srebnick, in *The Mysterious Death of Marie Rogers: Sex and Culture in Nineteenth-Century New York* (New York: Oxford Univ. Press, 1995), writes about Poe's fictionalization of the Mary Rogers murder case. Lively accounts of Helen Jewett's murder are available in Andie Tucher's *Froth and Scum: Truth, Beauty, Goodness, and the Ax Murder in America's First Mass Medium* (Chapel Hill: Univ. of North Carolina Press, 1994), Patricia Cline Cohen's *The Murder of Helen Jewett* (New York: Vintage, 1999), and David Anthony's "The Helen Jewett Panic: Tabloids, Men, and the Sensational Public Sphere in Antebellum New York," *American Literature* 69, no. 3 (1997): 487–514.

24. Isabelle Lehuu, *Carnival on the Page: Popular Print Media in Antebellum America* (Chapel Hill: Univ. of North Carolina Press, 2000), 37.

25. Erik S. Lunde, *Horace Greeley* (Boston: Twayne, 1981), 22.

26. Greeley, *Recollections of a Busy Life,* 137.

27. Qtd. in Mitchell, *Margaret Fuller's New York Journalism,* 16–17.

28. Margaret Fuller to Maria Rotsch, Sept. 25, 1844, in *The Letters of Margaret Fuller,* ed. Robert H. Hudspeth, vol. 3 of 6, *1842–1844* (Ithaca, NY: Cornell Univ. Press, 1984), 230.

29. Margaret Fuller to Samuel Ward, Dec. 29, 1844, *Letters of Margaret Fuller,* 3:256.

30. Chevigny, *Woman and the Myth,* 289.

31. On this point, see Betsy Klimasmith, *At Home in the City: Urban Domesticity in American Literature and Culture, 1850–1930* (Durham, NH: Univ. of New Hampshire Press, 2005), 3–7, who makes a convincing argument about the city as a space for public and private mingling in antebellum America.

32. Qtd. in von Mehren, *Minerva and the Muse,* 215.

33. Fuller, 1845 letter, *Letters of Margaret Fuller,* 4:39.

34. Janet Floyd, "Dislocations of the Self: Eliza Farnham at Sing Sing Prison," *Journal of American Studies* 40, no. 2 (2006): 311.

35. For more on antebellum prison reform, see Norval Morris and David J. Rothman, *Oxford History of the Prison: The Practice of Punishment in the Early Republic* (New York: Oxford Univ. Press, 1995); and Mark E. Kann, *Punishment, Prisons, and Patriarchy: Liberty and Power in the Early Republic* (New York: New York Univ. Press, 2005).

36. See, for instance, Carolyn L. Karcher, "Margaret Fuller and Lydia Maria Child: Intersecting Careers, Reciprocal Influences," in *Margaret Fuller's Cultural Critique: Her Age and Legacy,* ed. Fritz Fleischmann (New York: Peter Lang, 2000), 75–87, and Jennifer Greiman, "Theatres of Reform: Forms of the Public in Antebellum American Literature" (PhD diss., Univ. of California, Berkeley, 2003). Beginning in the 1830s, prostitution was a growing problem in New York, accompanying the city's rapid population growth. By 1840, within a metropolis of 310,000 residents, some 5,000–10,000 were prostitutes. See Patricia Cline Co-

hen, Timothy J. Gilfoyle, and Helen Lefkowitz Horowitz, *The Flash Press: Sporting Male Weeklies in 1840s New York* (Chicago: Univ. of Chicago Press, 2008), 7. For information about the climate of reform in 1840s America, see Belasco, "'The Animating Influences of Discord.'" We should note, however, Foucault's argument that since its inception, institutions of incarceration have been in a perpetual state of reform and "should not be seen as an inert institution" (Michel Foucault, *Discipline and Punish: The Birth of the Prison* [New York: Random House, 1977], 235). The 1840s reforms were but one of a long and continuous line of prison reform movements in America, so that many of the same arguments were rehearsed forty to fifty years later when Jordan and Bly wrote for the *New York World*.

37. Belasco, "Animating Influences of Discord," 76.

38. Thomas Hood, "Bridge of Sighs," *New-York Tribune*, June 19, 1845.

39. Margaret Fuller, "St. Valentine's Day—Bloomingdale Asylum for the Insane," *New-York Tribune*, Feb. 22, 1845. Pliny Earle, one of the founders of what was to become the American Psychiatric Association, was among a handful of doctors who, in the words of Roy Porter, "integrated medical and moral therapies in a climate of therapeutic optimism" (*Madness: A Brief History* [New York: Oxford Univ. Press, 2002], 110).

40. Fuller, "St. Valentine's Day—Bloomingdale Asylum for the Insane."

41. Margaret Fuller, "Our City Charities," *New-York Tribune*, Mar. 19, 1845.

42. Ibid.

43. Margaret Fuller to Maria Rotsch, Jan. 15, 1845, in *Letters of Margaret Fuller*, 4:46.

44. Fuller, "Our City Charities."

45. Jeffrey Steele, introduction to *The Essential Margaret Fuller*, ed. Jeffrey Steele (New Brunswick, NJ: Rutgers Univ. Press, 1992), xxxviii.

46. Fuller, "Our City Charities."

47. Margaret Fuller, "Asylum for Discharged Female Convicts," *New-York Tribune*, June 19, 1845.

48. Elizabeth Barnes, *States of Sympathy: States of Sympathy: Seduction and Democracy in the American Novel* (New York: Columbia Univ. Press, 1997), xi. See also Cindy Weinstein, *Family, Kinship, and Sympathy in Nineteenth-Century American Literature* (Cambridge: Cambridge Univ. Press, 2004) for a discussion of sentimentality and the boundaries of family.

49. Fuller, "Asylum for Discharged Female Convicts."

50. See, for instance, David S. Reynolds, *Beneath the American Renaissance: The Subversive Imagination in the Age of Emerson and Melville* (New York: Knopf, 1988), and Jesse Alemán and Shelley Streeby, eds., *Empire and the Literature of Sensation: An Anthology of Nineteenth-Century Popular Fiction* (New Brunswick, NJ: Rutgers Univ. Press, 2007).

51. Margaret Fuller, "French Novelists of the Day: Balzac . . . George Sand . . . Eugene Sue," *New-York Tribune*, Feb. 1, 1845.

52. Reynolds, *Beneath the American Renaissance*, 81, 85.

53. Fuller, "Asylum for Discharged Female Convicts."

54. Qtd. in Mitchell, *Margaret Fuller's New York Journalism,* 35–36.

55. Margaret Fuller, "Prison Discipline," *New-York Tribune,* Feb. 25, 1846.

56. Bean and Myerson, introduction to *Margaret Fuller, Critic,* xv, xxx.

57. Margaret Fuller, *Woman in the Nineteenth Century, Essential Margaret Fuller,* 329.

58. Fuller, "Our City Charities."

59. Harriet Beecher Stowe, *Uncle Tom's Cabin* (New York: Norton, 1994), 385.

60. Once she left New York, Fuller no longer drew a regular salary from the *Tribune,* receiving instead roughly $10 per column. See Annamaria Formichella Elsden, "Margaret Fuller's *Tribune* Dispatches and the Nineteenth-Century Body Politic," in *"The Only Efficient Instrument": American Women Writers and the Periodical, 1837–1916,* ed. Aleta Feinsod Cane and Susan Alves (Iowa City: Univ. of Iowa Press, 2001), 25; and Fink, "Margaret Fuller," 69.

61. Elsden, "Margaret Fuller's *Tribune* Dispatches," 27.

62. Steele, *Transfiguring America,* 238.

63. Margaret Fuller to Richard Fuller, Mar. 2, 1845, in *Letters of Margaret Fuller,* 4:54.

64. Qtd. in Capper, *Margaret Fuller, an American Romantic Life,* 213.

65. Qtd. in Mitchell, *Margaret Fuller's New York Journalism,* 33.

3. Entering Unceremoniously

1. Fanny Fern, *Ginger-snaps* (New York: Carleton, 1872), 115.

2. Lauren Berlant, "The Female Woman: Fanny Fern and the Form of Sentiment," *American Literary History* 3, no. 3 (1991): 430–31.

3. Although Sara Payson Willis was Fern's given name, I will refer to her throughout this chapter as "Fanny Fern," as the nom de plume essentially became her identity—even her grave marker bears the name "Fanny Fern." For a discussion of the marketing and copyrighting of "Fanny Fern" as a brand, see Melissa Homestead's "'Everybody Sees the Theft': Fanny Fern and Literary Proprietorship in Antebellum America," *New England Quarterly* 74, no. 2 (2001): 210–237.

4. See, for instance, Berlant, "Female Woman"; Jennifer Harris, "Marketplace Transactions and Sentimental Currencies in Fanny Fern's *Ruth Hall," American Transcendental Quarterly* 20 (2006): 343–59; and Martha J. Cutter, *Unruly Tongue: Identity and Voice in American Women's Writing, 1850–1930* (Jackson: Univ. Press of Mississippi, 1999). Jaime Harker notes that alongside Fern's "subversiveness and her humor" are sentimentalized "anthems to the God of nature and impassioned apologies for motherhood and religion" ("'Pious Cant' and Blasphemy: Fanny Fern's Radicalized Sentiment," *Legacy* 18, no. 1 [2001]: 52).

5. David Dowling, "Capital Sentiment: Fanny Fern's Transformation of the Gentleman Publisher's Code," *American Transcendental Quarterly* 22, no. 1 (2008): 347.

6. Qtd. in Fanny Fern, *Ruth Hall and Other Writings,* ed. Joyce W. Warren (New Brunswick, NJ: Rutgers Univ. Press, 1999), 215–16.

7. Nathaniel Hawthorne, *The Centenary Edition of the Works of Nathaniel Hawthorne,* vol. 17 of 23, *The Letters, 1853–1856* (Columbus: Ohio State Univ. Press, 1988), 307–8.

8. Joyce W. Warren, *Fanny Fern: An Independent Woman* (New Brunswick, NJ: Rutgers Univ. Press, 1992), 99. See page 109 for information on the marketing strategies Derby & Miller employed to increase sales of Fern's first book. Two more Derby & Miller contracts followed, for *Little Ferns for Fanny's Little Friends* (1854), and *Fern Leaves from Fanny's Portfolio,* 2d ser. ([Buffalo, NY: Miller, Orton and Mulligan, 1854]). Sales for all three books were indeed impressive. By 1854, according to Joyce Warren's accounting, some 180,000 copies had been sold in the United States and England; Warren details the phenomenal marketing campaign that bolstered sales of *Ruth Hall* in "Uncommon Discourse: Fanny Fern and the *New York Ledger,*" in *Periodical Literature in Nineteenth-Century America,* ed. Kenneth M. Price and Susan Belasco Smith (Charlottesville: Univ. Press of Virginia, 1995), 51–68.

9. Qtd. in Warren, *Fanny Fern,* 144.

10. Warren, "Uncommon Discourse," 59. One of Bonner's key strategies for increasing circulation was to turn his writers, beginning with Fern, into celebrities by employing massive advertising campaigns that played up their status. In essence, Fern and others became public figures on a grand scale. See ibid., 60–61; Homestead, "Everybody Sees the Theft"; and Ronald Weber, *Hired Pens: Professional Writers in America's Golden Age of Print* (Columbus: Ohio State Univ. Press, 1997), 52–55.

11. Fanny Fern, "Mistaken Philanthropy," *Olive Branch,* June 5, 1852.

12. Fanny Fern, "The Charity Orphans," *Olive Branch,* June 4, 1853.

13. Fanny Fern, "Whose Fault Is It?" *New York Ledger,* June 25, 1864. Certainly not every critic sees in Fern any kind of truly radical voice for change. Cori Brewster, for instance, in "Trading on the Exploited: Fanny Fern and the Marketplace Rhetoric of Social Justice," in *Popular Nineteenth-Century American Women Writers and the Literary Marketplace,* ed. Earl Yarington and Mary De Jong (Newcastle, UK: Cambridge Scholars Publishing, 2007), argues that Fern offers only "a rather narrow vision of social injustice and possible reforms" and therefore "does far more to contain challenges to existing power structures . . . than to advance such challenges herself" (239). Somewhat similarly, Stephen Hartnett argues that the novel is both "an exposé and a celebration of the cheerful brutality of capitalism" ("Fanny Fern's 1855 *Ruth Hall,* the Cheerful Brutality of Capitalism, and the Irony of Sentimental Rhetoric" *Quarterly Journal of Speech* 88, no. 1 [2002]: 1).

14. Fanny Fern, "The Working-Girls of New York," *New York Ledger,* Jan. 26, 1867.

15. Fanny Fern, *Fresh Leaves* (New York: Mason Brothers, 1856), 259.

16. Fern's writing here is a close echo of what Walt Whitman—whom Fern admired—writes in "Song of Myself": "The prostitute draggles her shawl, her bonnet bobs on her tipsy and pimpled neck, / The crowd laugh at her blackguard oaths, the men jeer and wink to each other, / (Miserable! I do not laugh at your oaths nor jeer you)" (*Leaves of Grass and Other Writings,* ed. Michael Moon [New York: Norton, 2002], ll. 302–4).

17. Fanny Fern, "Blackwell's Island No. 1," *New York Ledger,* Aug. 14, 1858.

18. Ibid.

19. Ibid.

20. Fanny Fern, "Blackwell's Island No. 3," *New York Ledger,* Aug. 24, 1854

21. Ibid.

22. Ibid.

23. "Misplaced Sympathy," *New York Ledger,* Apr. 5, 1856.

24. Fern, *Fern Leaves,* 358, 360, 359.

25. Fern, *Ginger-snaps,* 229–30, 231, 249.

26. Fanny Fern, "Blackwell's Island, No. II," *New York Ledger,* Aug. 21, 1858.

27. Ibid.

28. Warren, *Fanny Fern,* 125, 126.

29. Fern, *Ruth Hall and Other Writings,* 24.

30. Ibid., 3.

31. Ibid., 183.

32. Ibid., 50, 51.

33. Ibid., 109, 111.

34. Ibid., 109, 111, 112.

35. Ibid., 90, 3; Klimasmith, *At Home in the City.*

36. Fern, *Ruth Hall and Other Writings,* 90–91.

37. Ibid., 120.

38. Warren, *Fanny Fern,* 179. Richard Brodhead writes about such antebellum celebrity-seeking in *Cultures of Letters: Scenes of Reading and Writing in Nineteenth-Century America* (Chicago: Univ. of Chicago Press, 1995), 61–63.

39. Alison M. J. Easton, "My Banker and I Can Afford to Laugh! Class and Gender in Fanny Fern and Nathaniel Hawthorne," in *Soft Canons: American Women Writers and Masculine Tradition,* ed. Karen Kilkup (Iowa City: Univ. of Iowa Press, 1999), 222.

40. Harker, "Pious Cant," 57.

4. MAKING A SPECTACLE OF HERSELF

1. "Mrs. Halliday Not Insane," *New York Times,* Sept. 12, 1893.

2. Nellie Bly, "Nellie Bly Visits Mrs. Halliday," *New York World,* Oct. 22, 1893.

3. Ibid.

4. See Kerry Segrave, *Women and Capital Punishment in America, 1840–1899: Death Sentences and Executions in the United States and Canada* (Jefferson, NC: McFarland, 2008), 163–69.

5. Mark Bernhardt, "The Selling of Sex, Sleeze, Scuttlebutt, and Other Shocking Sensations: The Evolution of New Journalism in San Francisco, 1887–1900," *American Journalism* 28, no. 4 (2011): 113.

6. *World* headline dates from Jan. 4, 1898; Jan. 7, 9, 16, Feb. 10, Mar. 10, 1889.

7. "The Condemned Journalism," *Outlook*, Mar. 27, 1897.

8. Ibid.

9. Matthew Arnold, "Up to Easter," *Nineteenth Century* 21 (May 1887): 638.

10. "Condemned Journalism."

11. Tollen Smith, "New Journalism," *Life*, Oct. 28, 1897, 345.

12. "Condemned Journalism."

13. Elizabeth V. Burt, *Women's Press Organizations, 1881–1999* (Westport, CT: Greenwood, 2000), xii.

14. See also Michael Schudson, *Discovering the News: A Social History of American Thought and Culture, 1850–1920* (New York: Basic, 1978); Gerald J. Baldasty, *The Commercialization of News in the Nineteenth Century* (Madison: Univ. of Wisconsin Press, 1992); and Anne Varty, ed., *Eve's Century: A Sourcebook of Writings on Women and Journalism, 1895–1918* (London: Routledge, 2000), for accounts of the rise of this newly feminized commercial journalism.

15. "The Doings of Women Folk," *New York World*, Oct. 20, 1889.

16. Jean Marie Lutes, in *Front-Page Girls: Women Journalists in American Culture and Fiction, 1880–1930* (Ithaca, NY: Cornell University Press, 2006), and Alice Fahs in *Out on Assignment: Newspaper Women and the Making of Modern Public Space* (Chapel Hill: University of North Carolina Press, 2011), offer superb analyses of women's celebrity journalism in the late nineteenth century.

17. Edwin Shuman, *Steps into Journalism: Helps and Hints for Young Writers* (Evanston, IL: Evanston Press, 1894), 148. That same year, Margaret H. Welch made the same point in "Is Newspaper Work Healthful for Women? *Journal of Social Science* 32 (Nov. 1894): 110–16. See also E. A. Bennett's *Journalism for Women: A Practical Guide* (New York: John Lane, 1898), 11.

18. Shuman, *Steps into Journalism*, 148, 147, 150.

19. As with Fern, I will use Elizabeth Cochrane's nom de plume, Nellie Bly, with a nod to the fashion in which she *became* the newspaper character she had constructed. The spelling of the Pittsburgh paper (as of the city itself) at that time was indeed "Pittsburg."

20. Madelon Golden Schlipp and Sharon M. Murphy, *Great Women of the Press* (Carbondale: Southern Illinois Univ. Press, 1983), 136.

21. Brooke Kroeger, *Nellie Bly: Daredevil, Reporter, Feminist* (New York: Random House, 1994), 82. Kroeger nicely summarizes the discouraging remarks Bly encountered in her interviews with editors, 82–83.

22. Scholars disagree about the person responsible for the original idea of being locked up in an asylum, with some sources pinning credit on Pulitzer, some on Cockerill, and some (namely Bly herself) on Bly. Kroeger details the confusion about who was responsible for the asylum idea in *Nellie Bly*, 86.

23. See Julius Chambers, "The Lunacy Law Tested," *New-York Tribune,* Aug. 29, 1872; Chambers, "Abuses of Lunatics," *New-York Tribune,* Sept. 2, 1872; and Chambers, "More about Bloomingdale," *New-York Tribune,* Sept. 3, 1872.

24. "An Amateur Maniac" *Christian Union,* Oct. 9, 1884.

25. "An Escaped Lunatic," *Life,* Jan. 28, 1897.

26. Kroeger, *Nellie Bly,* 127, 87. Lutes has written the most comprehensive study of stunt reporters, in *Front Page Girls.*

27. Barbara Belford, *Brilliant Bylines: A Biographical Anthology of Notable Newspaper-Women in America* (New York: Columbia Univ. Press, 1986), 116.

28. Headlines from Oct. 30, 1887, Apr. 28, May 12, June 23, Aug. 18, 1889, Oct. 9, 16, 1887.

29. Nellie Bly, "Behind Asylum Bars," *New York World,* Oct. 9, 1887.

30. Ibid. Bly's equation of insanity with physical features would have been in keeping with medical opinion of the era, as well. At one point during her experience, for instance, a doctor declares her insane based on the appearance of her tongue and her heartbeat. Later another doctor calls her "insanity" into question, remarking that her "pulse and eyes were not that of an insane girl" (Nellie Bly, "Inside the Madhouse," *New York World,* Oct. 16, 1887).

31. Bly, "Behind Asylum Bars."

32. "Imprisoned with a Maniac," *New York World,* Jan. 12, 1889.

33. Bly, "Behind Asylum Bars."

34. Ibid.

35. Margaret Fuller, "St. Valentine's Day—Bloomingdale Asylum for the Insane," *New-York Daily Tribune,* Feb. 22, 1845.

36. Bly, "Behind Asylum Bars."

37. Bly, "Inside the Madhouse."

38. Ibid.

39. Ibid.

40. The echo between news articles and fictionalized tales is not random. As I discuss in *Narrating the News: New Journalism and Literary Genre in Late Nineteenth-Century American Newspapers and Fiction* (Kent, OH: Kent State Univ. Press, 2005), in the news market of the early 1890s, papers like the *New York World* positioned themselves in explicit competition with literary realism as they crafted stories that could be read against their fictional counterparts. In composing their own stories, reporters used such narrative frames as the detective tale, the travel adventure, and the historical romance, but they manipulated the framing to suggest that their stories were superior to the imaginary ones invented by writers of fiction. Although the entertainment-model newspapers were based on dramatic reportage, journalists on sensationalistic papers respected the influence of the rising "objectivity" and crafted stories that would resonate with truthfulness—or the illusion of it.

41. Edward Shorter, *History of Psychiatry: From the Era of the Asylum to the Age of Prozac* (Hoboken, NJ: Wiley, 1998), 113.

42. Bly, "Behind Asylum Bars."

43. Bly, "Inside the Madhouse."

44. Bly, "Behind Asylum Bars."

45. See also Kroeger, *Nellie Bly*, 91–92.

46. Qtd. in ibid., 91, 93.

47. The "medievalist," romantic flair is in keeping with the context in which Bly writes. The most popular and widely read subgenre of American fiction in the late 1880s and 1890s was the historical romance, often placed in castles and ruins.

48. Bly, "Behind Asylum Bars."

49. The asylum doctors are also labeled as inferior because of their inability to recognize Bly's acting in an October 15, 1887, *World* article, "All the Doctors Fooled."

50. "Nellie Brown's Story," *New York World*, Oct. 10, 1887. The front page of the *World* that day included another, unrelated, article of interest: "Insane Woman's Awful Death."

51. "All the Doctors Fooled."

52. Nellie Bly, "Untruths in Every Line," *New York World*, Oct. 17, 1887.

53. "Can Doctors Tell Insanity?" *New York World*, Oct. 23, 1887.

54. A curious modern parallel to Bly's undercover institutionalization lies in Norah Vincent's *Voluntary Madness: Lost and Found in the Mental Healthcare System* (New York: Penguin, 2009), which chronicles the author's attempts to have herself admitted to various mental wards and hospitals. Ultimately, Vincent's narrative becomes almost entirely self-referential, a work more about seeking sympathy for herself than about investigating the institutions themselves.

55. Nellie Bly, *Ten Days in a Mad-House* (New York N. L. Munro, 1887), 3, 6.

56. Ibid., 69–70.

57. Bly, "Inside the Madhouse."

58. Shorter, *History of Psychiatry*, 46.

59. Nellie Bly, "Nellie Bly a Prisoner," *New York World*, February 24, 1889.

60. Ibid.

61. We see another echo of this in an article about Bly's visit to a home for prostitutes, "In the Magdalen's Home" (*New York World*, Feb. 11, 1888), which starkly contrasts with a similar story by Fuller. Going undercover as a "public woman," a "woman of the streets," Bly spends one night in the home before deciding, as the epigraph to this chapter proclaims, "I had but little sympathy for these women who do wrong."

62. Another striking example is evident in the case of newspaper woman Kate Swan, who tried to see what one would feel as a woman on death row at New York's Dannemora Prison, going so far as to sit in the electric chair. Swan assumes the role of the sympathetic identifier, imagining herself "for the time a criminal. . . . I should never draw a breath of clean air again. I told myself all these things until in truth I could believe that I really was a miserable unfortunate with but an hour to live" ("A Woman in the Death Chair," *New York World*, Feb. 16, 1896). Ultimately, however, Swan's article serves as little more than a shocking read for both her and her readers.

63. Lutes, *Front-Page Girls*, 13.

5. Sympathy and Sensation

1. Elizabeth Jordan, "Tramped the Streets with a Corpse," *New York World,* Sept. 23, 1889.

2. Elizabeth Jordan, *Three Rousing Cheers* (New York: D. Appleton–Century, 1938), 37. The advice echoes a scene in *May Iverson's Career* (New York: Harper & Brothers, 1914), in which Iverson's mentor, a nun at the convent school Iverson attends, tells her, "When you write the sad stories you're so fond of . . . remember to let your readers shed their own tears" (5). Jordan was to follow this advice to success in her better fiction as well. A review of *Tales of the City Room* (New York: Scribner's, 1898), for instance, notes admiringly that Jordan is "stingy with tears," even as she expresses "keen sympathy" for her subjects (*Literary News* 19 [May 1898]: 145).

3. See Howard Good, *The Journalist as Autobiographer* (Metuchen, NJ: Scarecrow, 1993), 73; Maurine H. Beasley and Sheila J. Gibbons, *Taking Their Place: A Documentary History of Women and Journalism* (Washington, DC: American Univ. Press, 1993), 10; and Marion Marzolf, *Up from the Footnote: A History of Women Journalists* (New York: Hastings House, 1977), 26. The first women's press organization, the Ladies' Press Club of Washington, D.C., was formed in 1881 (see Elizabeth V. Burt, *Women's Press Organizations, 1881–1999* [Westport, CT: Greenwood, 2000]).

4. Ishbel Ross, *Ladies of the Press: The Story of Women in Journalism by an Insider* (New York: Harper, 1936), 2; Good, *Journalist as Autobiographer,* 75–76.

5. "Objectivity" was not a word used to describe journalism in the nineteenth century, but I use it here to refer to the principles of balance, thoroughness, and unbiased reporting that were already emerging at the end of the century. See David T. Z. Mindich, *Just the Facts: How "Objectivity" Came to Define American Journalism* (New York: New York Univ. Press, 1998), for a full account of the rise of journalistic objectivity.

6. For a thorough discussion of Jordan's composite novels, see June Howard, *Publishing the Family* (Durham, NC: Duke Univ. Press, 2001); Susanna Ashton, "Veribly a Purple Cow: *The Whole Family* and the Collaborative Search for Coherence," *Studies in the Novel* 33, no. 1 (2001): 51–79; and Elizabeth Freeman, "*The Whole(y) Family:* Economies of Kinship in the Progressive Era," *American Literary History* 16, no. 4 (2004): 619–47. Jordan collaborated with a number of other famous authors on two composite novels, *The Whole Family: A Novel* New York: Harper, 1908) and *The Sturdy Oak: The Sturdy Oak: A Composite Novel of American Politics* (New York: Henry Holt, 1917). The spelling of *Harper's Bazaar* was not to change until the twentieth century.

7. Kathleen A. Cairns, *Front-Page Women Journalists, 1920–1950* (Lincoln: Univ. of Nebraska Press), 8.

8. See, for instance, David Shi, *Facing Facts: Realism in American Thought and Culture, 1850–1920* (New York: Oxford Univ. Press, 1995), 216–20; Michael Davitt

Bell, *The Problem of American Realism: Studies in the Cultural History of a Literary Idea* (Chicago: Univ. of Chicago Press, 1993), 8; and Michael Robertson, *Stephen Crane, Journalism, and the Making of Modern American Literature* (New York: Columbia Univ. Press, 1997), 4.

9. Daniel H. Borus, *Writing Realism: Howells, James, and Norris in the Mass Market* (Chapel Hill: Univ. of North Carolina Press, 1989), 14, 173.

10. Henry James, "The Art of Fiction," in *The Art of Criticism: Henry James on the Theory and Practice of Fiction,* ed. William Veeder and Susan Griffin (Chicago: Univ. of Chicago Press, 1986), 173.

11. Qtd. in Donald Pizer, introduction to *Documents of American Realism and Naturalism,* ed. Donald Pizer (Carbondale: Southern Illinois Univ. Press, 1998), 7.

12. Shi, *Facing Facts,* 85.

13. Howard, *Publishing the Family,* 242. In the 1890s sentimentality found widespread expression in the form of historical romances, the most widely published and read novels of the decade. With ample melodrama and emotion, these novels "flooded American magazines and bookstores" during the last decade of the century—at least half of the best sellers published between 1894 and 1902 were "novels of high romance," in the words of Frank Luther Mott in in *Golden Multitudes: The Story of Best Sellers in the United States* (New York: Macmillan, 1947), 307, 311–12. See also Nancy Glazener, "Romances for 'Big and Little Boys': The U.S. Romantic Revival of the 1890s and James's *The Turn of the Screw,*" in *Cultural Institutions of the Novel,* ed. Deidre Lynch and William B. Warner (Durham, NC: Duke Univ. Press, 1996), 369–98.

14. Bell, *Problem of American Realism,* 177.

15. Elizabeth G. Jordan, *Tales of Destiny* (New York: Harper, 1902), 184, 260.

16. Jordan, *Three Rousing Cheers,* 17.

17. Ibid. 28, 29, 34–35.

18. Jordan's "Season of Outing" stories were composed for the Brooklyn edition of the *World* but recopied in the New York edition under the parenthetical byline "Special to the World," a mark that indicated she was not yet on the regular city staff.

19. Jordan, *Three Rousing Cheers,* 49. I discuss this column further in "'True Stories of the News,' and Newspaper Fiction in Late-Nineteenth-Century Journalism," in *Literature and Journalism: Inspirations, Intersections, and Inventions from Benjamin Franklin to Stephen Colbert,* ed. Mark Canada (New York: Palgrave Macmillan, 2013), 119–41.

20. Ross, *Ladies of the Press,* 177–78. Jordan sported her share of sensational, attention-getting articles, but she viewed herself as—and she was—a different kind of reporter than Bly, whom she saw as writing something other than hard news. See Jordan, *Three Rousing Cheers,* 23.

21. "Voices from the Tombs," *New York World,* Dec. 29, 1889.

22. Jordan, *Three Rousing Cheers,* 23.

23. Belford, *Brilliant Bylines: A Biographical Anthology of Notable Newspaper-Women in America* (New York: Columbia Univ. Press, 1986), 152.

24. Arthur Lubow, *The Reporter Who Would Be King* (New York: Scribner's, 1992), 26.

25. Jordan, "Ruth Herrick's Assignment," in *Tales of the City Room* (New York: Scribner's, 1898), 5, 6, 9–10.

26. Ibid., 23–24.

27. Ibid., 25.

28. Ibid., 27, 28.

29. Ibid., 12.

30. Ibid., 29.

31. Not all readers appreciated Jordan's perspective. Grumbled one reviewer of *Tales of the City Room,* "Why should Miss Jordan attempt to insinuate that it is only the woman reporter who can act humanely?" (*Public Opinion,* May 26, 1898, 665).

32. This is not to suggest that all other newspaper reporters lacked sympathy. Julian Ralph of the *New York Sun,* for instance, wove into his reportage a balanced commentary that asked readers to view the case carefully, as does Jordan's reporting. Still, other papers, perhaps most notably the *Boston Globe,* grossly sensationalized the case and framed Borden as a monster. And the local *Fall River Globe* was markedly anti-Borden and even published a rant against her every year on the anniversary of the murders.

33. The Lizzie Borden articles Jordan penned for the *New York World* include "The Case of Lizzie Borden" (June 4, 1893), "Lizzie Borden's Ordeal" (June 5, 1893), "Borden Jury Chosen" (June 6, 1983), "Miss Borden Faints" (June 7, 1893), "Borden Boomerangs" (June 8, 1893), "Lizzie's Dark Day" (June 9, 1893), "Miss Borden's Hope" (June 10, 1893), "In Favor of Lizzie" (June 11, 1893), "Lizzie Borden Fatigued" (June 12, 1893), "Going Lizzie's Way" (June 13, 1893), "Murders Re-Enacted" (June 14, 1893), "You Gave Me Away!" (June 15, 1893), "Lizzie's Side Heard" (June 16, 1893), "All the Evidence In" (June 17, 1893), "Borden Jurors Wrangle" (June 19, 1893), "This Is the Real Lizzie Borden" (June 18, 1893), "Lizzie Not over Anxious" (June 19, 1893), "A Plea for a Life" (June 20, 1893), and "Lizzie Borden Free" (June 21, 1893).

34. Elizabeth Jordan, "This Is the Real Lizzie Borden," *New York World,* June 18, 1893.

35. Ibid.

36. Ibid.

37. Elizabeth Jordan, "Miss Borden Faints," *New York World,* June 7, 1893.

38. Jordan, "Ruth Herrick's Assignment," 15.

39. Elizabeth Jordan, "Lizzie's Dark Day," *New York World,* June 9, 1893.

40. Ibid.

41. Jordan, "Miss Borden Faints."

42. Jordan, *Three Rousing Cheers,* 36.

43. Ibid.

44. Her editor's reaction is significant in terms of the development of women's newspaper writing, as described in the epilogue to this book: "Great Scott," he yells. "So you've joined the sobbing sisterhood at last!" Jordan, *May Iverson's Career,* 96, 97.

45. Ibid., 98, 104.

46. Ibid. 109.

47. Ibid. 110, 115, 119.

48. June Howard, "'Her Very Handwriting Looks as if She Owned the Earth': Elizabeth Jordan and Editorial Power," in *Women in Print: Essays on the Print Culture of American Women from the Nineteenth and Twentieth Centuries,* ed. Wayne A. Wiegand and Elizabeth Long (Madison: Univ. of Wisconsin Press, 2006), 65.

Afterword

1. Mildred Gilman, *Sob Sister* (New York: Grosset & Dunlap, 1931), 110, 246.

2. Ishbel Ross, *Ladies of the Press: The Story of Women in Journalism by an Insider* (New York: Harper, 1936), 65.

3. Gilman, *Sob Sister,* 19.

4. Patricia Bradley, *Women and the Press: The Struggle for Equality* (Evanston, IL: Northwestern University Press, 2005), 123, 12. Jean Marie Lutes's *Front-Page Girls: Women Journalists in American Culture and Fiction, 1880–1930* (Ithaca, NY: Cornell University Press, 2006), offers the definitive account of sob sister reporting. Other sources include Marzolf, *Up from the Footnote: A History of Women Journalists* (New York: Hastings House, 1977), 32; Phyllis Abramson, *Sob Sister Journalism* (Westport, CT: Greenwood, 1990), and George H. Douglas, *The Golden Age of the Newspaper* (Westport, CT: Greenwood, 1999), 182–87.

5. Gilman, *Sob Sister,* 146.

6. Lutes, *Front-Page Girls,* 4.

7. Douglas, *Golden Age of the Newspaper,* 188, 182.

Bibliography

Abramson, Phyllis. *Sob Sister Journalism*. Westport, CT: Greenwood, 1990.

Alamán, Jesse and Shelley Streeby, eds. *Empire and the Literature of Sensation: An Anthology of Nineteenth-Century Popular Fiction*. New Brunswick, NJ: Rutgers University Press, 2007.

"All the Doctors Fooled." *New York World*, October 15, 1887.

"An Amateur Maniac." *Christian Union*, October 9, 1884.

"An Escaped Lunatic." *Life*, January 28, 1897.

Anthony, David. "The Helen Jewett Panic: Tabloids, Men, and the Sensational Public Sphere in Antebellum New York." *American Literature* 69, no. 3 (1997): 487–514.

Arnold, Mathew. "Up to Easter." *Nineteenth Century* 21 (May 1887): 638.

Ashton, Susanna. "Veribly a Purple Cow: *The Whole Family* and the Collaborative Search for Coherence." *Studies in the Novel* 33, no. 1 (2001): 51–79.

Baldasty, Gerald J. *The Commercialization of News in the Nineteenth Century*. Madison: University of Wisconsin Press, 1992.

Barnes, Elizabeth. *States of Sympathy: Seduction and Democracy in the American Novel*. New York: Columbia University Press, 1997.

Bean, Judith Mattson, and Joel Myerson. *Margaret Fuller, Critic: Writings from the New-York Tribune, 1844–1846*. New York: Columbia University Press, 2000.

Beasley, Maurine H., and Sheila J. Gibbons. *Taking Their Place: A Documentary History of Women and Journalism*. Washington, DC: American University Press, 1993.

Belasco, Susan. "'The Animating Influences of Discord': Margaret Fuller in 1844." *Legacy* 20, nos. 1 & 2 (2003): 76–93.

Belford, Barbara. *Brilliant Bylines: A Biographical Anthology of Notable Newspaper-Women in America.* New York: Columbia University Press, 1986.

Bell, Michael Davitt. *The Problem of American Realism: Studies in the Cultural History of a Literary Idea.* Chicago: University of Chicago Press, 1993.

Bennett, E. A. *Journalism for Women: A Practical Guide.* New York: John Lane, 1898.

Bergman, Jill, and Debra Bernardi, eds. *"Our Sisters' Keepers": Nineteenth-Century Benevolence Literature by American Women.* Tuscaloosa: University of Alabama Press, 2005.

Berlant, Lauren. "The Female Woman: Fanny Fern and the Form of Sentiment." *American Literary History* 3, no. 3 (1991): 429–54.

Bernardi, Debra, and Jill Bergman, "Introduction: Benevolence Literature by American Women." In Bergman and Bernardi, *"Our Sisters' Keepers."* 1–19.

Bernhardt, Mark. "The Selling of Sex, Sleeze, Scuttlebutt, and Other Shocking Sensations: The Evolution of New Journalism in San Francisco, 1887–1900." *American Journalism* 28, no. 4 (2011): 111–42.

"Blackwell's Island." *American Magazine and Repository of Useful Literature,* April 1842, 67–69.

Blanchard, Paula. *Margaret Fuller: From Transcendentalism to Revolution.* New York: Delacorte, 1978.

Bly, Nellie. "Behind Asylum Bars." *New York World,* October 9, 1887.

———. "In the Magdalen's Home." *New York World,* February 12, 1888.

———. "Inside the Madhouse." *New York World,* October 16, 1887.

———. "Nellie Bly a Prisoner." *New York World,* February 24, 1889.

———. "Nellie Bly Visits Mrs. Halliday." *New York World,* October 22, 1893.

———. *Ten Days in a Mad-House.* New York: N. L. Munro, 1887.

———. "Untruths in Every Line." *New York World,* October 17, 1887.

———. "A Woman without a Heart." *New York World,* November 5, 1893.

Boardman, Samantha, and George J. Makari. "The Lunatic Asylum on Blackwell's Island and the New York Press." *American Journal of Psychiatry* 164, no. 4 (2007): 581.

Borus, Daniel H. *Writing Realism: Howells, James, and Norris in the Mass Market.* Chapel Hill: University of North Carolina Press, 1989.

Bradley, Patricia. *Women and the Press: The Struggle for Equality.* Evanston, IL: Northwestern University Press, 2005.

Brewster, Cori. "Trading on the Exploited: Fanny Fern and the Marketplace Rhetoric of Social Justice." In *Popular Nineteenth-Century American Women Writers and the Literary Marketplace,* edited by Earl Yarington and Mary De Jong, 236–49. Newcastle, UK: Cambridge Scholars Publishing, 2007.

Brodhead, Richard. *Cultures of Letters: Scenes of Reading and Writing in Nineteenth-Century America.* Chicago: University of Chicago Press, 1995.

Burt, Elizabeth V. *Women's Press Organizations, 1881–1999.* Westport, CT: Green-wood, 2000.

"By a Lunatic." "Insanity: Its Moral Treatment," *Phrenological Journal and Science of Health* (January 1874): 40–45.

Cairns, Kathleen A. *Front-Page Women Journalists, 1920–1950.* Lincoln: University of Nebraska Press, 2003.

"Can Doctors Tell Insanity?" *New York World,* October 23, 1887.

Capper, Charles. *Margaret Fuller, an American Romantic Life: The Public Years.* New York: Oxford University Press, 2007.

Cayton, Andrew R. L. "We Are All Nationalists, We Are All Localists." Review of David Waldstreicher, *In the Midst of Perpetual Fetes: The Making of American Nationalism, 1776–1820. Journal of the Early Republic* 18, no. 3 (1998): 521–28.

Chambers, Deborah, Linda Steiner, and Carole Fleming. *Women and Journalism.* London: Routledge, 2004.

Chambers, Julius. "Abuses of Lunatics." *New-York Tribune,* September 2, 1872.

———. "The Lunacy Law Tested." *New-York Tribune,* August 29, 1872.

———. "More about Bloomingdale." *New-York Tribune,* September 3, 1872

Chapman, Mary, and Glenn Hendler, eds. *Sentimental Men: Masculinity and the Politics of Affect in American Culture.* Berkeley: University of California Press, 1999.

Chevigny, Bell Gale. *The Woman and the Myth: Margaret Fuller's Life and Writings.* Rev. ed. Boston: Northeastern University Press, 1994.

Child, Lydia Maria. *Letters from New-York.* London: Richard Bentley, 1843.

Cohen, Patricia Cline. *The Murder of Helen Jewett.* New York: Vintage, 1999.

Cohen, Patricia Cline, Timothy J. Gilfoyle, and Helen Lefkowitz Horowitz. *The Flash Press: Sporting Male Weeklies in 1840s New York.* Chicago: University of Chicago Press, 2008.

"The Condemned Journalism." *Outlook,* March 27, 1897.

Cook, Sylvia Jenkins. *Working Women, Literary Ladies: The Industrial Revolution and Female Aspiration.* New York: Oxford University Press, 2008.

Cott, Nancy F. *The Bonds of Womanhood: Woman's Sphere in New England, 1780–1825.* New Haven: Yale University Press, 1977.

Coyle, Charles W. "Life in an Insane Asylum." *Overland Monthly and Out West Magazine* 21, no. 122 (February 1893): 161–71.

Cutter, Martha J. *Unruly Tongue: Identity and Voice in American Women's Writing, 1850–1930.* Jackson: University Press of Mississippi, 1999.

Davenport, W. H. "Blackwell's Island Lunatic Asylum." *Harper's New Monthly Magazine,* February 1866, 276–94.

De Forrest, Virginia. "Visit to a Lunatic Asylum—A True Sketch." *Lady's Home Magazine,* February 1858, 103–4.

De Jong, Mary G, and Paula Bernat Bennett, eds. *Sentimentalism in Nineteenth-Century America: Literary and Cultural Practices.* Madison, NJ: Fairleigh Dickinson University Press, 2013.

"Discomfiture of an Editress." *Frank Leslie's Illustrated Weekly,* September 3, 1859.

Dobson, Joanne. "Reclaiming Sentimental Literature." *American Literature* 69, no. 2 (1997): 263–88.

"The Doings of Women Folk." *New York World,* October 20, 1889.

Douglas, George H. *The Golden Age of the Newspaper.* Westport, CT: Greenwood, 1999.

Dowling, David. "Capital Sentiment: Fanny Fern's Transformation of the Gentleman Publisher's Code." *American Transcendental Quarterly* 22, no. 1 (2008): 347–64.

Easton, Alison M. J. "My Banker and I Can Afford to Laugh! Class and Gender in Fanny Fern and Nathaniel Hawthorne." In *Soft Canons: American Women Writers and Masculine Tradition,* edited by Karen Kilkup, 219–36. Iowa City: University of Iowa Press, 1999.

Elsden, Annamaria Formichella. "Margaret Fuller's *Tribune* Dispatches and the Nineteenth-Century Body Politic." In *"The Only Efficient Instrument": American Women Writers and the Periodical, 1837–1916,* edited by Aleta Feinsod Cane and Susan Alves, 23–44. Iowa City: University of Iowa Press, 2001.

"An Encounter with a Madman." *Cincinnati Weekly Herald and Philanthropist,* December 18, 1844.

The Englishman's Illustrated Guide Book to the United States and Canada. London: Longmans, Green, Reader, & Dyer, 1880.

Fahs, Alice. *Out on Assignment: Newspaper Women and the Making of Modern Public Space.* Chapel Hill: University of North Carolina Press, 2011.

"A Fellow-Passenger." *Youth's Companion,* May 29, 1879, 178–79.

Fern, Fanny. "Blackwell's Island No. 1." *New York Ledger,* August 14, 1854.

———. "Blackwell's Island No. II." *New York Ledger,* August 21, 1854.

———. "Blackwell's Island No. 3." *New York Ledger,* August 28, 1854.

———. "The Charity Orphans." *Olive Branch,* June 4, 1853.

———. *Fern Leaves from Fanny's Portfolio,* 2d. series. Buffalo, NY: Miller, Orton and Mulligan, 1854.

———. *Fresh Leaves.* New York: Mason Brothers, 1856.

———. *Ginger-snaps.* New York: Carleton, 1872.

———. "Mistaken Philanthropy." *Olive Branch,* June 5, 1852.

———. *Ruth Hall and Other Writings.* Ed. Joyce W. Warren. New Brunswick, NJ: Rutgers University Press, 1999.

———. "Whose Fault Is It?" *New York Ledger,* June 25, 1864.

———. "The Working-Girls of New York." *New York Ledger,* January 26, 1867.

Fink, Steven. "Margaret Fuller: The Evolution of a Woman of Letters." In *Reciprocal Influences: Literary Production, Distribution, and Consumption in America,* edited by Steven Fink and Susan S. Williams, 55–74. Columbus: Ohio State University Press, 1999.

Florence, Bella Rose. "The Maniac's Confession." *Peterson's Magazine* 33 (May 1858): 364–66.

Floyd, Janet. "Dislocations of the Self: Eliza Farnham at Sing Sing Prison." *Journal of American Studies* 40, no. 2 (2006): 311–25.

Foucault, Michel. *Discipline and Punish: The Birth of the Prison.* New York: Random House, 1977.

Franklin, Edward M. "The Madhouse, and Its Inmates." *Ballou's Dollar Monthly Magazine* 15, no. 1 (Jan. 1862): 79–80.

Freedman, Estelle B. *Their Sisters' Keepers: Women's Prison Reform in America, 1830–1930.* Ann Arbor: University of Michigan Press, 1984.

Freeman, Elizabeth. "The Whole(y) Family: Economies of Kinship in the Progressive Era." *American Literary History* 16, no. 4 (2004): 619–47.

Fuller, Margaret. "Asylum for Discharged Female Convicts." *New-York Daily Tribune,* June 19, 1845.

———. "Darkness Visible." *New-York Daily Tribune,* March 10, 1846.

———. *The Essential Margaret Fuller.* Ed. Jeffrey Steele. New Brunswick, NJ: Rutgers University Press, 1992.

———. "French Novelists of the Day: Balzac . . . George Sand . . . Eugene Sue." *New-York Daily Tribune,* February 1, 1845.

———. *The Letters of Margaret Fuller.* Ed. Robert H. Hudspeth. Vol. 3 of 6, *1842–1844.* Ithaca, NY: Cornell University Press, 1984.

———. *The Letters of Margaret Fuller.* Ed. Robert H. Hudspeth. Vol. 4 of 6, *1845–1847.* Ithaca, NY: Cornell University Press, 1987.

———. "Our City Charities." *New-York Daily Tribune,* March 19, 1845.

———. "Prison Discipline." *New-York Daily Tribune,* February 25, 1846.

———. "St. Valentine's Day—Bloomingdale Asylum for the Insane." *New-York Daily Tribune,* February 22, 1845.

Gamwell, Lynn and Nancy Tomes. *Madness in America: Cultural and Medical Perceptions of Mental Illness before 1914.* Ithaca, NY: Cornell University Press, 1995.

Gilman, Mildred. *Sob Sister.* New York: Grosset & Dunlap, 1931.

Glazener, Nancy. "Romances for 'Big and Little Boys': The U.S. Romantic Revival of the 1890s and James's *The Turn of the Screw.*" In *Cultural Institutions of the Novel,* edited by Deidre Lynch and William B. Warner, 369–98. Durham, NC: Duke University Press, 1996.

Good, Howard. *The Journalist as Autobiographer.* Metuchen, NJ: Scarecrow, 1993.

Goodman, Michael. *The Sun and the Moon: The Remarkable True Account of Hoaxers, Showmen, Dueling Journalists, and Lunar Man-Bats in Nineteenth-Century New York.* New York: Basic Books, 2008.

Gordon-Smith, George. "Psychological Sentimentalism: Consciousness, Affect, and the Sentimental Henry James." *Sentimentalism in Nineteenth-Century America: Literary and Cultural Practices,* edited by Mary G. De Jong and Paula Bernat Bennett, 181–96. Madison, NJ: Fairleigh Dickinson University Press, 2013.

Greeley, Horace. *Recollections of a Busy Life.* New York: J. B. Ford, 1868.

Greeson, Jennifer Rae. "The 'Mysteries and Miseries' of North Carolina: New York City, Urban Gothic Fiction, and *Incidents in the Life of a Slave Girl.*" *American Literature* 73 (June 2001): 277–309.

Greiman, Jennifer. "Theatres of Reform: Forms of the Public in Antebellum American Literature." PhD diss., University of California, Berkeley, 2003.

Halpern, Faye. *Sentimental Readers: The Rise, Fall, and Revival of a Disparaged Rhetoric.* Iowa City: University of Iowa Press, 2013.

Harker, Jaime. "'Pious Cant' and Blasphemy: Fanny Fern's Radicalized Sentiment." *Legacy* 18, no. 1 (2001): 52–64.

Harris, Jennifer. "Marketplace Transactions and Sentimental Currencies in Fanny Fern's *Ruth Hall*." *American Transcendental Quarterly* 20, no. 1 (2006): 343–59.

Hartnett, Stephen. "Fanny Fern's 1855 *Ruth Hall,* the Cheerful Brutality of Capitalism, and the Irony of Sentimental Rhetoric." *Quarterly Journal of Speech* 88, no. 1 (2002): 1–18.

Hawthorne, Nathaniel. *The Centenary Edition of the Works of Nathaniel Hawthorne,* vol. 17 of 23, *The Letters, 1853–1856.* Columbus: Ohio State University Press, 1988.

Hendler, Glenn. *Public Sentiments: Structures of Feeling in Nineteenth-Century American Literature.* Chapel Hill: University of North Carolina Press, 2001.

Homestead, Melissa. "'Everybody Sees the Theft': Fanny Fern and Literary Proprietorship in Antebellum America." *New England Quarterly* 74, no. 2 (2001): 210–37.

Hood, T. "A Tale of Terror." *Albion,* December 25, 1841, 455.

Hood, Thomas. "Bridge of Sighs." *New-York Tribune,* June 19, 1845.

"Hours in a Mad-House." *Christian Parlor Magazine,* April 1846, 367–71.

"How to See New York." *Scribner's Monthly,* June 1876, 272–74.

Howard, June. "'Her Very Handwriting Looks as if She Owned the Earth': Elizabeth Jordan and Editorial Power." In *Women in Print: Essays on the Print Culture of American Women from the Nineteenth and Twentieth Centuries,* edited by Wayne A. Wiegand and Elizabeth Long, 64–76. Madison: University of Wisconsin Press, 2006.

———. *Publishing the Family.* Durham, NC: Duke University Press, 2001.

———. "What Is Sentimentality?" *American Literary History* 11, no. 1 (1999): 63–81.

"Imprisoned with a Maniac." *New York World,* January 12, 1889.

"Insane Woman's Awful Death." *New York World,* October 10, 1887.

Irenaeus. "An Hour in an Insane Asylum." *New York Observer and Chronicle,* May 24, 1845.

———. "The Insane on Blackwell's Island." *New York Observer and Chronicle,* March 29, 1845.

James, Henry. *The Art of Criticism: Henry James on the Theory and Practice of Fiction.* Ed. William Veeder and Susan Griffin. Chicago: University of Chicago Press, 1986.

Jordan, Elizabeth G. "Lizzie's Dark Day." *New York World,* June 9, 1983.

———. *May Iverson's Career.* New York: Harper & Brothers, 1914.

———. "Miss Borden Faints." *New York World,* June 7, 1893.

———. "The Newspaper Woman's Story." *Lippincott's Monthly Magazine* 51 (March 1893): 340–47.

———. "Ruth Herrick's Assignment." In *Tales of the City Room,* 3–29. New York: Scribner's, 1898.

————. *Tales of Destiny.* New York: Harper, 1902.

————. "This Is the Real Lizzie Borden." *New York World,* June 18, 1893.

————. *Three Rousing Cheers.* New York: D. Appleton–Century, 1938.

————. "Tramped the Streets with a Corpse." *New York World,* September 23, 1889.

Jordan, Elizabeth, et al. *The Sturdy Oak: A Composite Novel of American Politics.* New York: Henry Holt, 1917.

————. *The Whole Family: A Novel.* New York: Harper, 1908.

Kann, Mark E. *Punishment, Prisons, and Patriarchy: Liberty and Power in the Early Republic.* New York: New York University Press, 2005.

Karcher, Carolyn L. "Margaret Fuller and Lydia Maria Child: Intersecting Careers, Reciprocal Influences." In *Margaret Fuller's Cultural Critique: Her Age and Legacy,* ed. Fritz Fleischmann, 75–87. New York: Peter Lang, 2000.

Keen, Suzanne. *Empathy and the Novel.* New York: Oxford University Press, 2007.

"A Keeper's Story." *Massachusetts Ploughman and New England Journal of Agriculture,* March 25, 1871.

Kerber, Linda K. "Separate Spheres, Female Worlds, Woman's Place: The Rhetoric of Women's History." *Journal of American History* 75, no. 1 (1988): 9–39.

Klimasmith, Betsy. *At Home in the City: Urban Domesticity in American Literature and Culture, 1850–1930.* Durham: University of New Hampshire Press, 2005.

Kopacz, Paula. "Feminist at the *Tribune:* Margaret Fuller as Professional Writer." *Studies in the American Renaissance* 20 (1991): 119–39.

Kroeger, Brooke. *Nellie Bly: Daredevil, Reporter, Feminist.* New York: Random House, 1994.

Lehuu, Isabelle. *Carnival on the Page: Popular Print Media in Antebellum America.* Chapel Hill: University of North Carolina Press, 2000.

Lewis, W. David. *From Newgate to Dannemora: The Rise of the Penitentiary in New York, 1796–1848.* Ithaca, NY: Cornell University Press, 1965.

Lubow, Arthur. *The Reporter Who Would Be King: A Biography of Richard Harding Davis.* New York: Scribner's, 1992.

Lunde, Erik S. *Horace Greeley.* Boston: Twayne, 1981.

Lutes, Jean Marie. *Front Page Girls: Women Journalists in American Culture and Fiction, 1880–1930.* Ithaca, NY: Cornell University Press, 2006.

"Madness in Novels." *Littell's Living Age,* April 21, 1866.

"Maniac Runs Amuck." *New York Times,* June 25, 1900.

"A Maniac's Deeds of Blood." *Chicago Daily Tribune,* June 20, 1887.

Marshall, David. *The Surprising Effects of Sympathy: Marivaux, Diderot, Rousseau, and Mary Shelley.* Chicago: University of Chicago Press, 1988.

Marzolf, Marion. *Up from the Footnote: A History of Women Journalists.* New York: Hastings House, 1977.

McGill, Meredith. *American Literature and the Culture of Reprinting, 1834–1853.* Philadelphia: University of Pennsylvania Press, 2002.

Meadows, Alice Maud. "The Romance of a Mad-House." *Once a Week,* February 2, 1892.

Miller, James. *Miller's New York As It Is.* New York: James Miller, 1880.

Mills, Kay. *A Place in the News: From the Women's Pages to the Front Page.* New York: Dodd, Mead, 1988.

Mindich, David T. Z. *Just the Facts: How "Objectivity" Came to Define American Journalism.* New York: New York University Press, 1998.

Miron, Janet. *Prisons, Asylums, and the Public: Institutional Visiting in the Nineteenth Century.* Toronto: University of Toronto Press, 2011.

"Misplaced Sympathy." *New York Ledger,* April 5, 1856.

Mitchell, Catherine C. *Margaret Fuller's New York Journalism: A Biographical Essay and Key Writings.* Knoxville: University of Tennessee Press, 1995.

Mitchinson, Wendy. "Gender and Insanity as Characteristics of the Insane: A Nineteenth-Century Case." *Canadian Bulletin of Medical History* 4, no. 2 (1987): 99–117.

Moore, H. H. "Sunday on 'The Island.'" *Christian Union,* October 11, 1883.

Morris, Norval, and David J. Rothman. *The Oxford History of the Prison: The Practice of Punishment in the Early Republic.* New York: Oxford University Press, 1995.

Mott, Frank Luther. *Golden Multitudes: The Story of Best Sellers in the United States.* New York: Macmillan, 1947.

"Mrs. Halliday Not Insane." *New York Times,* September 12, 1893.

Myerson, Joel. *The New England Transcendentalists and the Dial: A History of the Magazine and Its Contributors.* Madison, NJ: Fairleigh Dickinson Press, 1980.

"'Nellie Brown's' Story." *New York World,* October 10, 1887.

Nerone, John, and Kevin G. Barnhurst. "US Newspaper Types, the Newsroom, and the Division of Labor, 1750–2000." *Journalism Studies* 4, no. 4 (2003): 435–49.

"A Night with a Maniac." *Knickerbocker; or, New York Monthly Magazine* 5, no. 3 (March 1835): 221–30.

Nord, David Paul. *Communities of Journalism: A History of American Newspapers and Their Readers.* Urbana: University of Illinois Press, 2001.

Packer, Barbara. *The Transcendentalists.* Athens: University of Georgia Press, 2007.

Pasley, Jeffrey L. *"The Tyranny of Printers": Newspaper Politics in the Early American Republic.* Charlottesville: University of Virginia Press, 2001.

Porter, Roy. *Madness: A Brief History.* New York: Oxford University Press, 2002.

Pizer, Donald. Introduction to *Documents of American Realism and Naturalism,* ed. Donald Pizer, 3–17. Carbondale: Southern Illinois University Press, 1998.

Price, Kenneth M., and Susan Belasco Smith, eds. *Periodical Literature in Nineteenth-Century America.* Charlottesville: University Press of Virginia, 1995.

Reiss, Benjamin. *Theaters of Madness: Insane Asylums and Nineteenth-Century American Culture.* Chicago: University of Chicago Press, 2007.

Renner, Karen J. "Seduction, Prostitution, and the Control of Female Desire in Popular Antebellum Fiction." *Nineteenth-Century Literature* 65, no. 2 (2010): 166–91.

Reynolds, David S. *Beneath the American Renaissance: The Subversive Imagination in the Age of Emerson and Melville*. New York: Knopf, 1988.

Reynolds, Larry J. "From *Dial* Essay to New York Book: The Making of *Woman in the Nineteenth Century*." In Price and Smith, *Periodical Literature in Nineteenth-Century America*, 17–34.

Roberts, Heather. "'The Public Heart': Urban Life and the Politics of Sympathy in Lydia Maria Child's *Letters from New York*." *American Literature* 76 (December 2004): 749–75.

Robertson, Michael. *Stephen Crane, Journalism, and the Making of Modern American Literature*. New York: Columbia University Press, 1997.

Roggenkamp, Karen. *Narrating the News: New Journalism and Literary Genre in Late Nineteenth-Century American Newspapers and Fiction*. Kent, OH: Kent State University Press, 2005.

———. "'True Stories of the News,' and Newspaper Fiction in Late-Nineteenth-Century Journalism." In *Literature and Journalism: Inspirations, Intersections, and Inventions from Benjamin Franklin to Stephen Colbert*, edited by Mark Canada, 119–41. New York: Palgrave Macmillan, 2013.

Ross, Ishbel. *Ladies of the Press: The Story of Women in Journalism by an Insider*. New York: Harper, 1936.

Rothman, David J. *The Discipline of the Asylum: Social Order and Disorder in the New Republic*. Boston: Little, Brown, 1990.

Ryan, Mary P. *The Empire of the Mother: American Writing about Domesticity, 1830–1860*. New York: Harrington Park Press, 1985.

"A Sabbath Scene on Blackwell's Island." *Ladies' Repository*, December 1853, 552.

Sacks, Oliver. *Asylum: Inside the Closed World of State Mental Hospitals*. Cambridge: Massachusetts Institute of Technology Press, 2009.

Samuels, Shirley, ed. *The Culture of Sentiment: Race, Gender, and Sentimentality in Nineteenth-Century America*. New York: Oxford University Press, 1992.

Schlipp, Madelon Golden and Sharon M. Murphy. *Great Women of the Press*. Carbondale: Southern Illinois University Press, 1983.

Scholnick, Robert J. "'The Ultraism of the Day': Greene's *Boston Post*, Hawthorne, Fuller, Melville, Stowe, and Literary Journalism in Antebellum America." *American Periodicals* 18, no. 2 (2008): 163–91.

Schudson, Michael. *Discovering the News: A Social History of American Newspapers*. New York: Basic Books, 1978.

Segrave, Kerry. *Women and Capital Punishment in America, 1840–1899: Death Sentences and Executions in the United States and Canada*. Jefferson, NC: McFarland, 2008.

Shi, David. *Facing Facts: Realism in American Thought and Culture, 1850–1920*. New York: Oxford University Press, 1995.

Shorter, Edward. *A History of Psychiatry: From the Era of the Asylum to the Age of Prozac*. Hoboken, NJ: Wiley, 1998.

Shuman, Edwin. *Steps into Journalism: Helps and Hints for Young Writers.* Evanston, IL: Evanston Press, 1894.

Smith, Caleb. *The Prison and the American Imagination.* New Haven: Yale University Press, 2009.

Smith, Tollen. "New Journalism." *Life,* October 28, 1897.

Srebnick, Amy Gilman. *The Mysterious Death of Marie Rogers: Sex and Culture in Nineteenth-Century New York.* New York: Oxford University Press, 1995.

Steele, Jeffrey. *Transfiguring America: Myth, Ideology, and Mourning in Margaret Fuller's Writing.* Columbia: University of Missouri Press, 2001.

Stern, Julia A. *The Plight of Feeling: Sympathy and Dissent in the Early American Novel.* Chicago: University of Chicago Press, 1997.

Stowe, Harriet Beecher. *Uncle Tom's Cabin.* New York: Norton, 1994.

"Strangled by a Maniac." *New York Times,* October 11, 1897.

Swan, Kate. "A Woman in the Death Chair." *New York World,* February 16, 1896.

Review of *Tales of the City Room,* by Elizabeth Jordan. *Literary News* 19 (May 1898): 145.

Review of *Tales of the City Room,* by Elizabeth Jordan. *Public Opinion,* May 26, 1898.

Thomson, Rosemarie Garland. "Crippled Girls and Lame Old Women: Sentimental Spectacles of Sympathy in Nineteenth-Century American Women's Writing." In *Nineteenth-Century American Women Writers: A Critical Reader,* edited by Karen L. Kilkup, 128–45. Maiden, MA: Blackwell, 1998.

"The Tombs." *Prisoner's Friend,* October 1, 1849.

Tompkins, Jane. *Sensational Designs: The Cultural Work of American Fiction, 1790–1860.* New York: Oxford University Press, 1986.

Tracey, Karen. "Stories of the Poorhouse." In Bergman and Bernardi, *Our Sisters' Keepers,* 23–48.

"A Trip from Cincinnati to Cleveland and Detroit." *New-York Tribune,* June 19, 1844.

Tucher, Andie. *Froth and Scum: Truth, Beauty, Goodness, and the Ax Murder in America's First Mass Medium.* Chapel Hill: University of North Carolina Press, 1994.

Valente, Joseph. "The Novel and the Police (Gazette)." *Novel* 29, no. 1 (1995): 8–19.

Varty, Anne, ed. *Eve's Century: A Sourcebook of Writings on Women and Journalism, 1895–1918.* London: Routledge, 2000.

Vincent, Norah. *Voluntary Madness: Lost and Found in the Mental Healthcare System.* New York: Penguin, 2009.

"A Visit to the Lunatic Asylum on Blackwell's Island." *Harper's Weekly,* March 19, 1859.

"Voices from the Tombs." *New York World,* November 24, 1889.

Von Mehren, Joan. *Minerva and the Muse: A Life of Margaret Fuller.* Amherst: University of Massachusetts Press, 1994.

Warren, Joyce W. *Fanny Fern: An Independent Woman.* New Brunswick, NJ: Rutgers University Press, 1992.

———. "Uncommon Discourse: Fanny Fern and the *New York Ledger.*" In Price and Smith, *Periodical Literature in Nineteenth-Century America,* 51–68.

Way, Scott. "A Madman's Story." *Puck,* September 8, 1886.

Weber, Ronald. *Hired Pens: Professional Writers in America's Golden Age of Print.* Columbus: Ohio State University Press, 1997.

Weinstein, Cindy. *Family, Kinship, and Sympathy in Nineteenth-Century American Literature.* Cambridge: Cambridge University Press, 2004.

Welch, Margaret W. "Is Newspaper Work Healthful for Women?" *Journal of Social Science* 32 (November 1894): 110–16.

Welter, Barbara. "The Cult of True Womanhood: 1820–1860." *American Quarterly* 18, no. 2 (1966): 151–74.

———. *Dimity Convictions: The American Woman in the Nineteenth Century.* Athens: Ohio University Press, 1976.

"What Is Really Bad in Fiction." *American Builder and Journal of Art,* April 1, 1873.

Whitman, Walt. *Leaves of Grass and Other Writings.* Edited by Michael Moon. New York: Norton, 2002.

Whitt, Jan. *Women in American Journalism: A New History.* Urbana: University of Illinois Press, 2008.

Williams, Susan S. *Reclaiming Authorship: Literary Women in America, 1850–1900.* Philadelphia: University of Pennsylvania Press, 2006.

Index